The Future of
SCHOOL
CHOICE

*The Hoover Institution gratefully acknowledges
the following individuals and foundations for their
significant support of the*

Initiative
on
American Public Education

KORET FOUNDATION

TAD AND DIANNE TAUBE

TAUBE FAMILY FOUNDATION

LYNDE AND HARRY BRADLEY FOUNDATION

BOYD AND JILL SMITH

JACK AND MARY LOIS WHEATLEY

FRANKLIN AND CATHERINE JOHNSON

JERRY AND PATTI HUME

BERNARD LEE SCHWARTZ FOUNDATION

ELIZABETH AND STEPHEN BECHTEL JR. FOUNDATION

The Future of
SCHOOL
CHOICE

EDITED BY

Paul E. Peterson

HOOVER INSTITUTION PRESS
Stanford University   Stanford, California

www.hoover.org

Hoover Institution Press Publication No. 519

First printing 2003
09   08   07   06   05   04   03   9 8 7 6 5 4 3 2 1

Manufactured in the United States of America

The paper used in this publication meets the minimum requirements
of American National Standard for Information Sciences—Permanence
of Paper for Printed Library Materials, ANSI Z39.48-1984. ⊗

Library of Congress Cataloging-in-Publication Data
The future of school choice / Paul E. Peterson, editor.
        p.   cm.
   Includes bibliographical references and index.
   ISBN 0-8179-3952-0
   1. School choice—Law and legislation—United States.   2. Educational
vouchers—Law and legislation—United States.   I. Peterson, Paul E.
KF4137.F88 2003
379.1'11'0973—dc22   2003056770

Contents

Contributors

Peter Berkowitz
Associate Professor of Law, George Mason University
Research Fellow, Hoover Institution, Stanford University

Clint Bolick
Vice President and National Director of state chapters at
the Institute for Justice

Ronald Brownstein
National political correspondent, *Los Angeles Times*,
based in Washington, D.C.

Louis R. Cohen
Partner of Wilmer, Cutler & Pickering

Charles L. Glenn
Professor of Educational Policy
Fellow of the University Professors Program,
Boston University

C. Boyden Gray
Partner of Wilmer, Cutler & Pickering

Steven K. Green
> Associate Professor, Willamette University
>> College of Law

Jan De Groof
> Professor, Collège d'Europe, Brussels, Belgium
> President of the European Association for Education Law
> and Policy (ELA)

Bryan Hassel
> Co-Director of Public Impact, an education policy
> consulting firm

Terry M. Moe
> Professor of Political Science, Stanford University
> Senior Fellow, Hoover Institution

Paul E. Peterson
> Henry Lee Shattuck Professor of Government and
>> Director of the Program on Education Policy and
>> Governance, Harvard University
> Senior Fellow, Hoover Institution
> Editor-in-Chief of *Education Next: A Journal of Opinion*
> *and Research*

Kenneth W. Starr
> Partner at Kirkland & Ellis in their Washington, D.C.,
> office
> Adjunct Professor, New York University
> Distinguished Visiting Professor, George Mason
>> University Law School

Martin R. West
> Research Associate in the Program on Education Policy
> and Governance, Harvard University

Preface

School vouchers, tax credits, charter schools, the right to leave failing schools—all are concepts hardly known as recently as fifteen years ago. Though propounded as early as 1955 by Hoover scholar Milton Friedman, these ideas did not gain currency until 1990 when another Hoover scholar, Terry Moe, together with John Chubb, published a book, *Politics, Markets, and Public Schools,* that showed how politics undermined effective public education. Also that year, the State of Wisconsin established a small voucher program in Milwaukee, shortly after a charter initiative had been enacted by the State of Minnesota. Both ideas have since cascaded across the nation.

With the spread of the choice idea has come intense opposition, especially from vested interests with a stake in existing institutional arrangements. Virtually every effort to increase choice and competition in education has met stern resistance from teachers unions, established school boards, and most state departments of education.

Much of the antagonism to choice has expressed itself in the courtroom. School vouchers were said to be unconstitutional, because they violated the First Amendment ban on the establishment of religion. But it remained unclear whether school vouchers actually "established" a religion, or simply permited the "free exercise thereof," a right also protected by the First Amendment. In 2002, the Supreme Court, in *Zelman v. Simmons-Harris*, answered this question by saying that no constitutional violation occurs as long as voucher programs take a neutral stance, allowing students a choice of a religious or secular school.

Does this decision open the door to large-scale school choice? Or will choice programs in the future be as small and scattered as those that have thus far been tried? Will school choice simply become the latest fad to be given a trial run, only then to be abandoned? Or are the small steps taken thus far harbingers of an educational future quite unlike the present?

Much hangs on the answer to this question. American education, for at least a half century, has been stagnant, excessively bureaucratized, overrun by special groups and vested interests, unable to respond to the changing dynamic of society as a whole. The problem is not to be solved by adding more dollars to the equation, by teaching fewer students in each class, or by creating a few school-choice boutiques.

In this volume, the authors consider whether something more substantial might be occurring. They examine the meaning of the recent Supreme Court decision and consider the new political and policy context it has created. Our authors do not provide any single answer as to the future of school choice, though all acknowledge the manifold obstacles the movement must overcome. Yet there is a certain implied optimism, a sense that this movement, unlike past school reform fads, is likely to press forward, simply because choice, once granted, is seldom withdrawn. Once parents exercise it, they love choice dearly, all but ensuring its perpetuation.

All but one of the papers in this volume were initially presented at an October 2002 conference hosted by Harvard University's Program on Education Policy and Governance. These papers have been strengthened by the comments and discussion of the participants in that conference, including Alan Altshuler, Cory Booker, John Brandl, Chester Finn Jr., Jay Greene, Michael Owens, Bruce Manno, David Steiner, Joseph Viteritti, and Patrick Wolf. In addition to the conference papers, the volume includes an essay by Ronald Brownstein on the implementation of the choice provisions contained in the 2002 education law, *No Child Left Behind*. The essay originally appeared as "Locked Down: Will Failing Public Schools Let Students Leave?" *Education Next* 3 (summer 2003): 40–47. The introduction to this volume includes material that appeared originally in Paul E. Peterson, "Victory for Vouchers?" *Commentary* 114 (September 2002): 46–50.

The conference was supported by a grant from the John M. Olin Foundation. Antonio Wendland, the Associate Director of PEPG, provided invaluable assistance with the organization of the conference and the preparation of this volume. Mark Linnen assisted in this effort. Christopher Berry helped prepare some of the essays for publication. I am especially grateful to John Raisian, director of the Hoover Institution, for his help in seeing that these papers are made available to a broader audience. I also wish to thank the staff of the Hoover Institution Press, who assisted with the production of this volume, including Pat Baker, Marshall Blanchard, Jeff Bliss, Lyn Larson, and Richard Sousa.

Introduction
After
Zelman v. Simmons-Harris,
What Next?

PAUL E. PETERSON

In the most anticipated decision of its 2002 term, the Supreme Court ruled, in the case of *Zelman v. Simmons-Harris*, that the school voucher program in Cleveland, Ohio, did not violate the Constitution's ban on the "establishment" of religion. Opponents of vouchers—that is, the use of public funds to help low-income families pay tuition at private schools, including religious schools—were predictably disappointed, but pledged to fight on. As Senator Edward M. Kennedy declared, "Vouchers may be constitutional," but "that doesn't make them good policy."

The policy's sympathizers, needless to say, saw the ruling in a different light. President George W. Bush used the occasion of the Supreme Court's decision to issue a full-throated endorsement of vouchers. *Zelman*, he told a gathering in Cleveland, did more than remove a constitutional cloud; it was a "historic" turning point in how Americans think about education. In 1954, in *Brown v. Board of Education*, the Court had ruled that the country could not have two sets of schools, "one for African-Americans and one for whites." Now, the president continued, in ruling as it did in the Cleveland case, the Court was affirming a similar principle, proclaiming that "our nation will not accept one education system for those who can afford to send their children to a school of their choice and one for those who can't." *Zelman*, according to the President, is *Brown* all over again.

But is it? That question forms the core issue addressed in this collection of papers, most of which were initially presented at a conference hosted by the Program on Education Policy and Governance at Harvard University in October 2002. Part One of the volume looks at the legal meaning of *Zelman*, assessing whether its legal impact is broad or narrow. Part Two explores the broader political and policy context in the wake of this Supreme Court decision. Altogether, the collection as a whole provides an overview of the direction in which the school choice movement is likely to go in the years ahead.

Publicly funded school vouchers got their start in Milwaukee, Wisconsin, in 1990. Established at the urging of local black leaders and Wisconsin Governor Tommy Thompson (now Secretary of Health and Human Services), the program was originally restricted to secular private schools and included fewer than a thousand needy students. To accommodate growing demand, religious schools were later allowed to participate, an arrangement declared constitutional in 1998 by the Wisconsin Supreme Court. The Milwaukee program now provides a voucher worth up to $5,785 each to over 10,000 students, amounting to more than 15 percent of the school system's eligible population.

In 1999, at the behest of Governor Jeb Bush, Florida also established a publicly funded voucher program, aimed at students attending public schools that failed to meet state standards. Though only a few hundred students were participating in the failing-school program in 2003, another 9,000 students were participating in a separate voucher program for those found to be in need of special education. The failing-school program in Florida is also noteworthy because it served as a model for the voucher-like federal scholarship program advocated by George W. Bush during the 2000 presidential campaign.

Though the Milwaukee and Florida programs received the most public attention, it was the program in Cleveland that finally reached the writing desk of the Chief Justice. The Cleveland program is relatively small, providing in 2003 a maximum of $2,750 a year to each of roughly 5,000 students. Parents use the vouchers overwhelmingly for religious schools, which in recent years have matriculated over 90 percent of the program's participants. This, according to lawyers for the teachers unions, the most powerful foe of vouchers, constituted an obvious violation of the separation between church and state. The unions prevailed twice in federal court, winning decisions at the trial and appellate level against Susan Zelman, Ohio's superintendent of public instruction and the official responsible for administering the Cleveland program.

But the Supreme Court, in a 5–4 decision, was not persuaded. In his opinion for the majority in *Zelman*, Chief Justice William Rehnquist pointed to three well-known precedents— *Mueller* (1983), *Witters* (1986), and *Zobrest* (1993)—in which the Court had allowed government funds to flow to religious schools. What these cases had in common, Chief Justice Rehnquist wrote, and what they shared with the Cleveland voucher program, was that public money reached the schools "only as a result of the genuine and independent choices of private individuals." Under Cleveland's program, families were in no way coerced to send their children to religious schools; they had a range of state-funded options, including secular private schools, charter schools, magnet schools, and traditional public schools. As Kenneth W. Starr points out in the opening essay below, Rehnquist concluded that the voucher program was "entirely neutral with respect to religion."

The dissenters in *Zelman*, led by Justice David Souter, challenged the majority's reading of the relevant precedents—especially of *Nyquist* (1973), a ruling that struck down a New York State program giving aid to religious schools—and suggested that the choice in Cleveland between religion and non-religion was a mere legal fiction. They saved their most pointed objections, however, for what they saw as the likely social consequences of the ruling. The Court, Souter wrote, was promoting "divisiveness" by asking secular taxpayers to support, for example, the teaching of "Muslim views on the differential treatment of the sexes," or by asking Muslim Americans to pay "for the endorsement of the religious Zionism taught in many religious Jewish schools." Justice Stephen Breyer suggested that the decision would spark "a struggle of sect against sect," and Justice John Paul Stevens wondered if the majority had considered the lessons of other nations' experience around the world, including "the impact of religious strife . . . on the decisions of neighbors in the Balkans, Northern Ireland, and the Middle East to mistrust one another."

In his essay below, Peter Berkowitz reflects on the vitriol contained within these comments, pointing out that there is little in the practice of religious schools in the United States that justifies such language. Moreover, most of the world's democracies fund both religious and secular schools without causing undue domestic turmoil. In their essay on the way in which the religious issue is handled in other countries, Charles L. Glenn and Jan De Groof show that tensions can be managed without bitter, divisive controversy.

Still, if judicial rhetoric is all that counts, the dissenters in *Zelman* had the better of it. In the majority opinion, by contrast, there is very little that rises to the level of *Brown*'s often-cited language about the demands of American equality. Even observers pleased by the ruling were disappointed that the majority's opinion did not go much beyond showing how the facts of the case fit past precedents; there are no ringing declarations in Chief Justice Rehnquist's stodgy prose. In fact, the decision may have been a narrow one, hardly in the same league as *Brown*. In two separate essays, Stephen K. Green as well as Louis R. Cohen and C. Boyden Gray suggest that *Zelman* may have been a more narrow decision than some believe. In Cleveland, vouchers were accompanied by charter schools (called community schools in Ohio) and other forms of school choice, which give parents a range of secular options that accompanied the religious ones obtained through vouchers. They point out that it is not altogether clear whether voucher initiatives are unconstitutional in the absence of a significant range of secular choices.

Still, in separate concurring opinions written by two of the Justices one gets a sense of the wider issues at stake. Responding to the worries of the dissenters, Justice Sandra Day O'Connor pointed out that taxpayer dollars have long flowed to various religious institutions—through Pell Grants to denominational colleges and universities; through child-care subsidies that can be used at churches, synagogues, and other religious institutions; through direct aid to parochial schools for transportation, textbooks, and other materials; and, indirectly, through the tax code, which gives special breaks to the faithful. If government aid to religious institutions were such a problem, she suggested, wouldn't American society be torn already by sectarian strife?

As Peter Berkowitz points out, several well-designed studies have shown that students who attend private schools in the U.S. are not only just as tolerant of others as their public school peers but are also *more* engaged in political and community life. Catholic schools have a particularly outstanding record, probably because for more than a century American Catholics have felt compelled to teach democratic values as proof of their patriotism. There are obviously some extremists, but there is no reason to doubt that most of the country's religious schools are attempting to prove that they, too, can create good citizens.

As for *Brown* itself, only Justice Clarence Thomas, in his own stirring concurrence, pointed to it as an explicit precedent, quoting Frederick Douglass to argue that today's inner-city public school systems "deny emancipation to urban minority students":

> The failure to provide education to poor urban children perpetuates a vicious cycle of poverty, dependence, criminality, and alienation that continues for the remainder of their lives. If society cannot end racial discrimination, at least it can arm minorities with the education to defend themselves from some of discrimination's effects.

For Justice Thomas, as for President Bush, whose own remarks were undoubtedly influenced by these passages, vouchers are a civil rights issue; they promise not to intensify religious strife, as the Court's dissenters would have it, but to help heal the country's most enduring social divide.

Whether *Zelman* can in fact meet these high expectations remains very much to be seen. *Brown*, in principle, was self-enacting. Neither state legislatures nor local school boards could defy the ruling without running afoul of the law. George Wallace, Bull Conner, and many other Southern politicians were willing to do just that, but in the end, federal authorities imposed the Supreme Court's decision on the vested interests that opposed it.

Zelman is different. Though it keeps existing voucher programs intact, it does not compel the formation of new ones. Here the barricades to change remain extraordinarily high.

When *Brown* was handed down, Northern public opinion was moving against segregation; on the issue of vouchers, by contrast, public opinion is highly uncertain. Pollsters can get either pro-voucher or anti-voucher majorities simply by tinkering with the wording of their questions and the order in which they are asked. Nor, despite greater exposure for the issue, have the public's views evolved much in recent years; questions asked in 1995 generated basically the same results in 2000.

Vouchers suffer from more serious problems among members of the political class. As Terry M. Moe discusses in his essay on voucher politics, at both national and state levels, substantial bipartisan support is usually necessary to get a piece of legislation through the various committees, past a vote in two chambers, and signed into law. For vouchers, such support has never materialized. Whatever the private opinions of Democrats, for most of them it is political suicide to support vouchers publicly. Teachers unions have long placed vouchers at the top of their legislative kill list, and they are a key Democratic constituency, providing the party with both substantial financing and Election Day shock troops.

Nor can voucher proponents rely on wholehearted support from the GOP. Most Republicans, especially social conservatives and libertarians who have read their Milton Friedman, support vouchers in principle. Still, an idea whose primary appeal is to black Americans, the most faithful of all Democratic voting blocs, is a hard sell among the Republican rank-and-file. Vouchers simply do not have much resonance with well-heeled suburbanites who already have a range of educational choices. When vouchers came up as state ballot questions in both California and Michigan two years ago, most

Republican politicians found a way to dodge the issue—and the proposals lost badly.

Even if this political situation were to change, most states have constitutional restrictions of their own that may be invoked to scuttle attempts to provide vouchers for use at religious schools. Many of these provisions are the so-called "Blaine" amendments, dating to the nineteenth century, when James G. Blaine, a Senator from Maine and a Republican presidential candidate, sought to win the anti-immigrant vote by campaigning to deny public funds to Catholic schools. (Blaine is perhaps most famous for describing the Democrats as the party of "Rum, Romanism, and Rebellion.") In its classic version, the Blaine amendment read as follows:

> No money raised by taxation for the support of public schools, or derived from any public fund therefor, nor any public lands devoted thereto, shall ever be under the control of any religious sect; nor shall any money so raised or lands so devoted be divided between religious sects or denominations.

In a number of cases, Clint Bolick tells us in his essay below, state courts have interpreted Blaine amendments to mean nothing more than what is required, according to the Supreme Court, by the establishment clause of the First Amendment. In this interpretation, vouchers are safe—but not every state judge necessarily shares this opinion. In Florida, an appeals court has overturned a trial court decision that found that Florida's voucher program runs afoul of the state constitution.

Although the Florida case may persist in state courts for some time to come, the issue may appear before the U.S. Supreme Court in a quite different case as early as 2004, when the Court is expected to decide *Davey v. Locke.* This case arose because the State of Washington relied partly on its Blaine amendment to revoke the publicly funded scholarship of a student, Joshua Davey, who decided to major in theology at Northwest College. An appeals court found this interpretation of the Washington constitution in violation of the federal constitution. If the U.S. Supreme Court upholds the appeals court, it may neutralize the Blaine amendments altogether, thereby clearing the legal path for school vouchers.

But even if school vouchers should falter on state constitutional grounds, that would not necessarily forestall the school choice movement. Three other avenues remain under active consideration—tax credits, charter schools, and public school choice—though each contains its own set of speed bumps and potholes.

Several states, including Minnesota, Arizona, Florida, and Pennsylvania, are experimenting with tax credits and tax deductions, reducing taxes by a portion of the amount one pays for school tuition, or by what one contributes toward private school scholarships. In some forms, private school tax credits and deductions are indistinguishable from vouchers, the only difference being the distribution of funds to parents via the tax code rather than by the grant-making authority of government. To many economists, this is a legal distinction without substantive meaning. But in the world of law and practice, says Martin R. West in his essay below, state tax credits and deductions are quite different. For one thing, their constitutional validity is much more difficult to challenge, having stood tests in both state and federal courts. For another, they are more popular with the general public, winning higher levels of support than vouchers in opinion polls. Many private school operators also prefer tax credits and deductions, because they are less likely to be accompanied by governmental strings. On the other hand, it is more difficult to target tax credits and deductions toward disadvantaged populations. Much of the equal opportunity élan that has motivated the voucher movement might be lost, were this to become the sole form of school choice.

Charter schools, schools run under government charters by private entities, have gained even broader acceptability than tax credits and tax deductions. As many as thirty-six states have allowed the formation of charter schools, though in many states the law restricts charter school operations in important ways, either by limiting the number of charter schools or by placing them under the authority of potentially hostile regulatory agencies. But according to Bryan Hassel, in his essay below, the idea has been popular enough that, as of 2003, almost 685,000 students, better than one percent of the school-age population, were attending over 2,700 charter schools. The period of rapid growth occurred in the mid to late 1990s; since 2000, the growth rate has tapered off in the face of strengthened union opposition, tighter regulatory controls, and a series of well-publicized scandals at a few charter schools.

Hassel points out that the charter system has one important advantage over school vouchers: it addresses the supply side of the school choice equation. Although vouchers may give parents the wherewithal to pay for private schools, that means little unless private schools increase in number, or expand in size. Yet the initial costs of starting a new school, and recruiting a constituency for the school, can be very large. With a charter from the state in hand, charter school operators are better placed to open a new school. Also, charter schools have typically received an amount close to that received for the operating costs of public schools, something not available through most existing voucher programs. But even with these advantages, charter schools still face many practical and political problems that can be addressed only if they receive greater encouragement from public officials and if they develop their own networks of support and sharing of information. Hassel identifies useful ways in which progress can be made.

Finally, there is the public school choice encouraged under the recent federal legislation, No Child Left Behind, enacted into law in January 2002. The legislation says that any failing school must allow students to attend other public schools within the school district. It remains unclear whether this nationwide choice provision will open the door to a wide set of school choices. According to Ronald Brownstein, local school districts have done little to implement the legislation in the first year that it has taken effect; in time, groups may form to spur more effective implementation of the law, but skeptics will wonder whether a choice among traditional public schools is enough for those trapped within the inner core of our large metropolitan areas.

Depending on the way in which these issues are addressed, the Court's famed ruling in *Zelman* could still make the decision as critical as *Brown*. Certainly, the pro-choice movement, like the desegregation movement, means much more for minority students and their families than for other Americans.

For decades, and despite a host of compensatory reforms, the sizable gap in educational performance between blacks and whites has remained roughly the same. According to the National Assessment of Educational Progress, black eighth graders continue to score about four grade levels below their white peers on standardized tests. Nor is this gap likely to close as long as we have, again in President Bush's words, "one education system for those who can afford to send their children to a school of their choice and one for those who can't."

When parents choose a neighborhood or town in which to live, they also select, sometimes quite deliberately, a school for their children, often relying on various Internet services and real-estate agents for information about test-score data and other pertinent details about school districts and even individual schools. But there is a catch: the mobility that makes these choices possible costs money. It is no accident that children lucky enough to be born into privilege also attend the nation's best schools.

African Americans are often the losers in this arrangement. Holding less financial equity, and still facing discrimination in the housing market, they choose from a limited set of housing options. As a result, their children are more likely to attend the worst public schools. Richer, whiter districts rarely extend anything more than a few token slots to low-income minority students outside their communities.

It is therefore not surprising that blacks have benefited most when school choice has been expanded. In multi-year evaluations of private voucher programs in New York City, Washington, D.C., and Dayton, Ohio, my colleagues and I found that African American students, when given the chance to attend private schools, scored significantly higher on standardized tests than comparable students who remained in the public schools. In New York, where estimates are the most precise, those who switched from public to private schools scored, after three years, roughly 8 percentage points higher on math and reading tests than their public school peers, a difference of about two grade levels. If reproduced nationwide, this result would cut almost in half the black-white test score gap. (Interestingly, there is no evidence that vouchers have improved the academic performance of students from other ethnic groups. In my own research, they had no impact, positive or negative, on the test scores of either whites in Dayton or Hispanics in New York City.)

These findings about the especially positive effects of private schools on African American students are hardly isolated.

One review of the literature, conducted by the Princeton economist Cecilia Rouse, concludes that even though it is difficult to discern positive benefits for white students, "Catholic schools generate higher test scores for African Americans." Another, done by Jeffrey Grogger and Derek Neal, economists from the University of California at Los Angeles and the University of Chicago, respectively, finds little in the way of detectable gains for whites but concludes that "urban minorities in Catholic schools fare much better than similar students in public schools."

We do not know precisely what accounts for the gains that black students have made by switching to private schools. The answer is certainly not money, since the private schools they attend are usually low-budget, no-frills operations. The most striking difference, according to the research conducted by William Howell, Patrick Wolf, David Campbell, and myself, lies in the general educational environment: the parents of these students have reported being much more satisfied with everything from the curriculum, homework, and teacher quality to how the schools communicate with the parents themselves. The classes tend to be smaller, they say, and there is less fighting, cheating, racial conflict, or destruction of property.

No Child Left Behind

But how about those students left behind in traditional public schools? Even if students attending private schools are better off, will not those remaining in public schools be adversely affected? Like Caesar's Gaul, this question can be divided into three parts. Do vouchers attract the best and brightest from public schools? Does the performance of public schools spiral downward? Do public schools lose critically important fiscal resources? Let's consider each part separately.

Do Vouchers Attract the Best and the Brightest?

My own research has looked at the question of "the best and the brightest" in two different ways. In one study, my colleagues and I compared a random sample of all those who applied for a voucher offered nationwide by the Children's Scholarship Fund with a national cross-section of all those eligible to apply. African American students were twice as likely to apply as others. Specifically, 49 percent of the applicants were African American, even though they constituted just 26 percent of the eligible population. Other results reveal little sign that the interest in vouchers is limited to only the most talented. On the contrary, voucher applicants were just as likely to have a child who had a learning disability as all those in the eligible population. Nor is it only the better educated families who take an interest. Twenty-three percent of the mothers of applicants said they had graduated from college, as compared with 20 percent of the mothers in the eligible population.

In a second study, this time of vouchers in New York, Washington, D.C., and Dayton, my colleagues and I looked at those who actually made use of a voucher when it was offered to them. We did not find any evidence that private schools discriminated on the basis of a young student's test-score performance at the time they received an application from a voucher recipient. Among young applicants in New York City and Washington, D.C., there was no significant difference in the test scores at the time of application between voucher users and those who turned down the voucher and remained in public school. In Dayton, those using the voucher actually had lower math scores at the time of application, showing even more clearly that private schools were willing to take the educationally challenged student. Only among older students (grades 6–8) in Washington, D.C., did we see some signs that private schools expected students to meet a minimum educational standard prior to admission.

Other researchers find much the same pattern. In Milwaukee, the Wisconsin Legislative Audit Bureau found that the ethnic composition of the participants in Milwaukee's voucher program during the 1998–1999 school year did not differ materially from that of students remaining in public schools. Similarly, a University of Wisconsin evaluation of an earlier, smaller voucher program in Milwaukee found few consistent test-score or family-background differences between those who took vouchers and those who remained in public schools. In Cleveland, Indiana University analysts said that voucher "students, like their families, are very similar to their public-school counterparts." In short, vouchers tend to recruit a cross-section of the families and students eligible for participation.

Upon reflection, these findings are not particularly surprising. Families are more likely to want to opt out of a school if their child is doing badly than if the child is doing well. A number of families, moreover, select a private school because they like the religious education it provides, or because it is safe, or because they like the discipline. When all these factors operate simultaneously, the type of student who takes a voucher usually looks little different from those who pass up the opportunity.

Public School Performance

If vouchers do not simply pick off the top students within the public schools, but instead attract a cross-section of students, then there is no obvious educational reason why public schools should suffer as a result of the initiative. On the contrary, public schools, confronted by the possibility that they could lose substantial numbers of students to competing schools within the community, might well pull up their socks and reach out more effectively to those they are serving. Interestingly enough, there is already some evidence that public schools do exactly that.

Harvard economist Caroline M. Hoxby has shown, for example, that since the Milwaukee voucher program was established on a larger scale in 1998, it has had a positive impact on public school test scores. The public schools in the low-income neighborhoods most intensely impacted by the voucher program increased their performance by a larger amount than scores in areas of Milwaukee and elsewhere in Wisconsin not affected by the voucher program. She also found a similar positive impact of charter school competition on public school test scores in Michigan and Arizona, the two states in the country with the largest number of students attending charter schools. In other words, when substantial numbers of students are using vouchers or going to charter schools, public schools in the vicinity apparently respond by improving their educational offerings and, as a result, public school performance is enhanced.

Even the threat of a voucher can have a positive effect on test scores. Research by Manhattan Institute scholar Jay Greene shows that when public schools were in danger of failing twice on the statewide Florida exam, making their students eligible for vouchers, these public schools made special efforts to avoid failure. Their test scores climbed more than did almost equally bad schools (which had D-minus test scores) that were not threatened by vouchers. Greene was able to rule out the possibility that the improvements were the result of the additional resources made available to the F schools. In other words, competition—even the threat of competition—had positive effects in Florida.

One way to look at the impact of choice on public schools over the long run is to compare student performance across metropolitan areas that have varying numbers of private schools. The greater the number of private schools, the greater the competition, and the greater the impact on public schools. If the presence of private schools undermines public schools, then one expects to find lower public school performance in metropolitan areas where private schools abound. But a Harvard study has shown exactly the opposite: public school students do better in those parts of the country where there is more ready access to private schools. Similarly, some metropolitan areas have more school districts than others, giving parents the option to choose among different public school systems by moving to the neighborhood of choice. Knowing that this sort of parental choice can affect community property values, school boards seem to respond by providing parents better quality education. Research shows that this in fact happens, that in metropolitan areas with more school districts, students are given more demanding academic courses, school sports are given less emphasis, costs are reined in, and students learn more.

Fiscal Impacts on Public School Children

To see how school vouchers affect the fiscal resources available to public school children, the structure of public school financing needs to be briefly considered. Although the financial arrangements vary from one state to the next, on average, nationwide, 49 percent of the revenue for public elementary and secondary schools comes from state governments, 44 per-

cent is collected from local sources, and the balance comes in
the form of grants from the federal government. Most of the
revenue school districts get from state governments is distributed on a "follow the child" principle. The more students in a
district, the more money it receives from the state. If a child
moves to another district, the state money follows the child.
Local revenue, most of which comes from the local property
tax, stays at home, no matter where the child goes. As a result,
if a district suffers a net loss of students, the amount of money
the district has per pupil actually increases, simply because
local revenues can now be spread over fewer pupils.

The voucher programs in Milwaukee, Cleveland, and Florida have been designed along similar lines. The state money
follows the child, but the local revenue stays behind in local
public schools, which means that more money is available per
pupil. In Milwaukee, per-pupil expenditures for public school
children increased by 22 percent between 1990 and 1999, rising from $7,559 to $9,036. Not all of the increase was a direct
result of the voucher program, but the case disproves any claim
that students in public schools necessarily suffer from fewer
financial resources when voucher programs are put into effect.

Though voucher programs have been designed in such a
way as to be fiscally advantageous to public school children,
future central-city programs should do more. They should be
designed in such a way as to enhance resources available to
public and private schools alike. If funds for public schools are
greatly enhanced, public schools will be given every opportunity to respond effectively to the competition private schools
pose. And given the competition, public schools will have
strong incentives to make effective—and efficient—use of the
extra monies. At the same time, vouchers that are much larger
than those currently available will attract new entrepreneurs
to education, both nonprofits and for-profits. Existing private

schools will be as challenged as public schools by new, energetic educators.

The Future of School Choice

Until now, all voucher programs have been limited to students from low-income families. Although this may have been appropriate for initial demonstration programs, a larger program should not encourage segregation of students by income. Instead, programs should be designed to encourage integration in both public and private schools, economically as well as socially. For this to happen, vouchers need to be generally available.

A citywide voucher program may also attract some of the middle and working class families who left cities because of the low quality of the urban schools. Gentrification has restored a number of urban neighborhoods in a few parts of the country, but city life has proved mainly attractive to those who need not worry about school quality—the young and the retired. Unfortunately, many couples leave the city they enjoy simply because they cannot bear the thought of placing their children in a public school—and a private school is beyond their means. Vouchers would provide an option for such families. If enough are enticed into remaining in the city, schools will gradually become better integrated, and central cities will be revitalized.

Still, the key to change lies within the black community, and especially with parents, who increasingly know that private schools provide a better education for their children. A 1998 poll by Public Agenda, a nonpartisan research group, found that 72 percent of African American parents supported vouchers, as opposed to just 59 percent of white parents. A poll conducted two years later by the Joint Center for Political and Economic Studies had similar results, with just under half of the overall adult population supporting vouchers but 57 percent of African American adults favoring them. Perhaps more to the point, blacks constituted nearly half of all the applicants for the 40,000 privately funded vouchers offered nationwide by the Children's Scholarship Fund in 1999, even though they comprised only about a quarter of the eligible population.

Even in the face of such numbers, it is too much to expect that men like Jesse Jackson and Al Sharpton will reconsider their virulent opposition to vouchers; their political tendencies are too well defined. But pressure to support school vouchers is building among black parents, and black leaders will have to respond. Howard Fuller, the former superintendent of Milwaukee's public school system, has formed the Black Alliance for Educational Options, a pro-voucher group that has mounted an effective public relations campaign and is making waves in civil rights circles.

Not even the Supreme Court, it should be recognized, can make educational change come quickly in America. Though *Brown* was handed down in 1954, it took more than a decade before major civil rights legislation was enacted; southern schools were not substantially desegregated until the 1970s. Anyone writing about *Brown* ten years after its passage might have concluded that the decision was almost meaningless except for a few border states.

The question now is whether the ruling in *Zelman* will have any greater near-term impact than *Brown* did. Like *Brown* the Court's authoritative pronouncement on the constitutionality of vouchers has already conferred new legitimacy on those calling for reform. Newspaper editors and talk-show hosts have been forced to give the idea more respect, and political opponents cannot dismiss it so easily. Still, just as *Brown* did not produce immediate results, the same may be said about

Zelman. Perhaps the safest prediction is that, in four or five decades, American education will have been altered dramatically, in ways we cannot anticipate, by the parental demand for greater choice—a demand codified in *Zelman.* Many battles will be fought and lost along the way, to be sure, but the victories will accumulate, because choice, once won, is seldom conceded.

PART ONE

Zelman v. Simmons-Harris

—

Constitutional and Philosophical Implications

1

The Equality Principle

KENNETH W. STARR

Zelman v. Simmons-Harris has certainly changed the school choice landscape. But to see exactly just what has transpired, we should first look at the meaning of Zelman itself. I want to make two basic points, one that focuses on facts and contexts, the other that is more analytical or theoretical.

It was Justice Lewis Brandeis who said quite famously: "facts, facts, facts. Give me facts, don't give me theory." Without embracing a Brandeisian contextualism, I think it is helpful in understanding Zelman, and then school choice as a public policy issue more broadly, to look at the specific factual context that gave rise to the Zelman case. In doing so, I draw upon the Supreme Court's majority opinion, which provides key facts about Cleveland and its public school system.

The Court observes that the Cleveland public school system was placed into receivership by a federal district court judge who had been asked to oversee the desegregation of the Cleveland schools. The judge appointed the state superintendent as essentially the superintendent of schools of Cleveland. Was this just an instance of runaway judicial power or was the school system truly deficient? Maybe a little bit of both, but consider these disheartening facts: (1) the district had failed to make any of eighteen state standards for minimal acceptable performance; (2) only one-in-ten ninth graders could pass a basic proficiency examination; (3) students at all levels performed, in the Court's words, at a "dismal rate compared with students in other Ohio public schools"; (4) more than two-thirds of high school students either dropped out or failed before graduation. There are many more facts such as these. Now this contextual background suggests that this one pilot project that made it all the way to the Supreme Court of the United States was a bipartisan response by the political apparatus of Ohio—both by the state legislature and by two governors (Voinovich and Taft)—to a judicially mandated takeover of the Cleveland school system.

It is useful in this context to compare Cleveland's situation with the school choice program in Milwaukee, which began in 1990 and expanded in 1995 to include religiously affiliated schools. This, too, was a pilot choice program but it was not initiated in response to a judicial mandate or injunction. Instead, Milwaukee's voucher program grew out of a grass-roots political reaction guided by a reform-minded Republican governor and a progressive Democratic mayor. It was thoroughly bipartisan. It had deep support within the community, including business leaders from more than one religious faith.

As a final contextual point, consider private philanthropy in the school choice arena, which developed concurrently with the Milwaukee program. Across the country, men and women of goodwill, of all political persuasions, or of no political persuasion at all, found the state of education so abysmal with respect to inner-city students that they offered to give these students a choice. Some were quite opposed to the idea of publicly financed choice but they were willing to put literally millions of dollars of their own money into providing privately financed scholarships because of the hopelessness of those children in the schools of America's inner cities. These developments form the context for the *Zelman* case.

Let me now turn to a more theoretical or analytical point. The Chief Justice's reasoning in *Zelman* is straightforward, quite predictable for those who are student's of Rehnquist's legal jurisprudence. Intriguingly, the Chief Justice draws from case law not involving inner-city social and educational collapse, but from a series of opinions involving what can fairly and accurately be described as middle class entitlement cases. Most important, there were the big three: *Mueller v. Allen* (1983), *Witters v. Washington Department of Services for the Blind* (1986), and *Zobrest v. Catalina Foothills School District* (1993). Let's consider them in turn.

Mueller, from Minnesota, involved a tax deduction program—not a particularly lively area of debate in the inner city. This was a middle class entitlement program, even though 96 percent of its benefits went to the parents of children in religiously affiliated schools. The Supreme Court nonetheless upheld the program, saying statistical percentages were not what counted in constitutional matters.

Witters, from the state of Washington, involved a young man aspiring to enter the ministry. He was suffering from a disability and applied to the Washington Educational Rehabilitation Authorities for a scholarship so that he could become a pastor. The Supreme Court of Washington State ruled against the aspiring pastor, arguing that the Establishment Clause—the separation of church and state—would not permit the use of public funds to attend religious schools. The Supreme Court of the United States reversed by a margin of 9–0, with not a single justice in dissent. The Court ruled that Mr. Witters could choose to use his scholarship at a religious institution.

The third case is *Zobrest,* from Arizona. Larry Zobrest was deaf. His parents could afford tuition at a Catholic high school, but they wanted their son to be able to bring with him an already extant state-provided and federally funded sign-language interpreter. The Supreme Court of the United States upheld the program. The decision was not unanimous, but the principle was clear: because the interpreter was present in the religious school as a result of private choice—as opposed to government direction—there was no constitutional problem.

In light of that jurisprudential background spanning fifteen years, the Court did not struggle in reaching a decision in the *Zelman* case. There was no hand-wringing, no sense that this case required an exception to a general rule. The opinion does set forth the abysmal facts of educational failure in the Cleveland schools, but there is not a hint in the opinion that this was decisive to the judicial analysis. The Court simply looked at its own precedents and found a ready answer.

As everyone who follows the Court knows, this is a Court that takes its precedents very seriously. Whatever one may think about a particular jurisprudential strain, this is the Court that thought *Roe v. Wade* was wrongly decided but re-embraced it. It thought *Miranda* was wrongly decided but re-embraced it. But the *Zelman* decision was about more than grudgingly following precedent. Rather, it affirmed with enthusiasm a clear *principle* drawn from those cases that were identified as controlling.

The *Zelman* decision arose from a deeply unifying principle developed in the cases of neutrality and private choice. But those are technical words. The word at the heart of this decision is *equality*. Neutrality, after all, is just an expression of equality. The power of the equality principle for this Court is quite noteworthy. It is shown by reference to the Court's work in the free speech area, which set the stage. In still another

landmark case, *Widmar v. Vincent*, a small Christian group at
the University of Missouri, Kansas City, wanted to meet on
campus. But the university said *no*, invoking the separation
principle and the Establishment Clause. The case went to
the Supreme Court of the United States. The ruling, an 8–1
decision, was that the university cannot discriminate. The
University must treat all groups equally. It cannot single out
a group and exclude them from the public square because
of the particular viewpoint that they are articulating and
embracing.

Widmar was really the fountainhead for the equality principle, though it was not widely recognized at the time the decision was handed down. This decision, made twenty-one years
ago, set forth the equality principle—the principle essentially
of nondiscrimination—and it crowned the equality principle
the winner over the separation principle. I give you this pro-
vocative thought: separationism died in *Widmar* twenty-one
years ago as a unifying principle of the Court's work, but people were very slow to discover its death. What the Court did
in *Widmar* was not a sort of balancing act. There was to the
Court a *right answer* and only one answer, and it was the *equality answer*. In other words, there is a principle—equality—and
when we apply it we get an answer as if we were in the world
of mathematics. It is very simple: Do not exclude. Stop the
discrimination. This is obviously a principle of enormous
power. When we focus on that principle, we see that, in terms
of what is ahead, the Supreme Court has given school choice
a very bright green light.

The equality principle lifts up high values of great moral
appeal—inclusiveness and community. The equality principle, not surprisingly, was embraced very shortly after *Widmar*
at a political level by the Congress of the United States, by
overwhelming bipartisan majorities, in the Equal Access Act.

The Equal Access Act stopped the discrimination at high schools against Bible study clubs. If a school allows the chess club or the French club to meet, it must also allow Bible study clubs, prayer groups and the like.

The constitutionality of the Equal Access Act was tested in the Supreme Court a few years later in the *Bridget Mergens* case. The Board of Education of Westside, outside Omaha, Nebraska, would not allow a Bible study club to meet in the school. Ms. Mergens hired a lawyer and the lawyer invoked the Equal Access Act. The *Mergens* decision was 8–1: the Bible study club could meet at the school. Equality triumphed over separationism. Only Justice Stevens was in dissent. Interestingly enough, in that dissent he did not rest his view on separationism principles. He grounded his dissent entirely on federalism principles, arguing that Congress did not intend to intrude so deeply into the administration of local school districts. But Stevens was a small minority; for the Court as a whole, separationism was over.

Despite this, four justices dissented from *Zelman*. In the main dissenting opinion, Justice Souter tried mightily to steer himself around these various tributes to the equality principle. He searched in a very lawyer-like way, very diligently and earnestly, and he found an answer: the separationist principle embodied in the Supreme Court's opinion in the 1950s called *Everson v. The Board of Education of the Township of Ewing, New Jersey.* But there was a problem, and Justice Souter—able lawyer and justice that he is—recognized it. *Everson* seemed to embrace separationism, but, concretely, the decision itself did a very different thing. *Everson* came down against aid to religious schools but then proceeded to allow aid to religious schools in the context of bus transportation. So Justice Souter turned to the notion of *substantiality*. Public funding may be used for bus transportation and various aid programs, but the aid cannot be *too substantial.* Justice Souter recognized that *no aid* does not really mean *no aid.* He realized that *Muller, Witters,* and *Zobrest* must stand for something. But, according to Justice Souter, these cases do not permit substantial aid for religious institutions. Souter's effort at explaining the cases went on for more than thirty pages. (The word "lugubrious" springs to mind.) But there was an enormous roadblock standing in Justice Souter's way, set up in 1986 by that judicial moderate, Louis F. Powell Jr., in his opinion in *Witters,* which clarified issues left unresolved in *Widmar.*

In *Widmar,* where the opinion was written by Justice Thurgood Marshall, the Court concluded that a public scholarship to attend a religious school is similar to taking a paycheck from the government and turning it over to a religious organization: perfectly acceptable. There is no suggestion that *substantial* aid in Washington is going to support people studying for the ministry. So Justice Marshall concluded that there is no need to worry: *de minimis non curat lex.* He rests his opinion more on the minimum effect doctrine than on the free choices of the individuals involved. However, if there had been substantial aid going to seminaries, it is not so clear how the case might have been decided.

But, in *Witters,* Justice Powell provided a more convincing rationale for voucher-like arrangements. According to Powell, it does not matter how many citizens choose to use public aid at a religious institution. This is not a direct grant to a religious institution—it is indirect through the medium of private choice. That was really a watershed that takes us beyond *Widmar.* Justice Powell, in *Witters,* garnered five votes not just for the decision, but, even more important, to go beyond Justice Marshall's *de minimis* stance to one focused on private choice.

Among those who agreed with Justice Powell was Justice Sandra Day O'Connor. She did not join his opinion but she

expressed in a separate opinion her view that Justice Powell
was right. Justice Sandra Day O'Connor is the bellwether of the
Rehnquist Court—as she goes, so goes the Court. Justice
O'Connor is ardently committed to the equality principle in a
variety of settings. She responded in *Zelman* quite elaborately
to Justice Souter and his colleagues and said, in effect, that the
interconnections between faith communities and the government are so legion and of such considerable vintage that it
makes no sense to have the pretense of permitting no public
aid. Justice O'Connor has a remarkable ability, and has had
over time, to find a position that seems to resonate quite
strongly with the common sense of the American people. She
is pragmatically attached to what works and avoids rigid doc-
trines, whether of the ideological left or of the right. She has
spoken against grand unified theories because they may turn
out to be not so grand and not so unified. Yet, on school choice,
she is solidly in the equality camp—for solid pragmatic as well
as theoretical reasons.

So what does this mean for litigation that is under way in
Florida and Maine? What about those Blaine amendments to
some state constitutions, whose origins date back to a period
of virulent anti-Catholicism? People should be ashamed to be
wrapping themselves in the cloak of Senator James G. Blaine,
the nineteenth-century opponent of schools built by Catholic
immigrants. Self-proclaimed liberals need to pick another
hero. He cared much more for the exclusion of immigrants than
he did for equality of opportunity. So today, whenever judges
rely on these state Blaine amendments as a way of denying
school choice, as a Florida trial court has recently done, these
judges find themselves in real tension with the equality principle.

Think about the way in which the equality principle works
in higher education. Are we going to tell the G.I. returning from

Kandahar and Tora Bora, "Sorry, you can't go to Notre Dame, it's too religious"? The idea that you can't use government funds to go to an institution of your choice seems quite silly now. Wisely, the separationists tend to look the other way when it comes to the G.I. Bill.

Instead, they seek more vulnerable targets: vouchers for inner-city children, for instance. Yet there really is something morally unattractive about telling an otherwise qualified needy family that they cannot use available funds to send their child to a school that fosters values of their faith community. There is, in short, a difference between (1) parents' being unable to choose a religiously affiliated school because they do not have the means, and (2) the state's giving the parents the means but then limiting the choices available. The former involves choices naturally influenced and shaped by economics; the latter involves choices being shaped, if not directed, by government.

I close by returning briefly to *Everson*. *Everson* talked the talk of separationism, but then it fell back and embraced a principle that it called neutrality, a form of equality. The Court explained that it would be wrong to tell the citizens of Everson Township that if they chose to provide bus transportation to public school children they could not provide it to Catholic school children or other religiously affiliated children. While policing the Establishment Clause, the Court must be "sure"— the words of Hugo Black—"that we do not inadvertently prohibit New Jersey from extending its general State law benefits to *all its citizens* without regard to their religious belief [my italics]." And there it is. It was in *Everson* all along. The word "all"—of inclusiveness, of full membership in the community, of nondiscrimination.

It should now be clear that, quite apart from moral considerations, it is at least problematic constitutionally for the state to exclude religious persons, groups, or institutions from otherwise neutral programs. With *Zelman* building on the big three of *Mueller*, *Witters*, and *Zobrest*, has the bell tolled for programs that, in response to state separationist principles, say "we hereby exclude?" *Zelman* tells us now that it is over. You cannot discriminate. The well-designed choice program is the inclusive choice program.

2

Seminal
or
Symbolic?

STEVEN K. GREEN

The litigation road to the Supreme Court's decision in *Zelman v. Simmons-Harris* was long and tortuous.[1] Filed initially in 1996, the case wound its way slowly through the Ohio and federal courts, eliciting rulings that favored both sides in the controversy. Going into the Supreme Court arguments in February 2002, the plaintiffs had prevailed in four out of five lower court decisions. But as we all know, the final decision is all that matters in the world of constitutional litigation, and voucher proponents can take great satisfaction in their victory. For one point is clear: the Supreme Court—albeit by the narrowest of margins—held that vouchers for private religious schools, as represented in the Cleveland Scholarship Program, are constitutional under the Establishment Clause.[2]

Yet the *Zelman* decision may tell us little else, particularly about how the Court would rule on a differently constructed voucher program or, more immediately, whether voucher-like programs will withstand challenges brought under state laws.

1. 122 S. Ct. at 2460 (2002).
2. Id. at 2473.

That long and winding road to *Zelman* may thus look more like an expressway in comparison to the next round of voucher litigation.

I wish to make three points in response to Kenneth Starr's observations about the *Zelman* holding. First, I wish to give my analysis of the holding as one of the attorneys who challenged the Cleveland program. Second, I will discuss the significance of the holding, which can be viewed in some respects as a seminal ruling, while in other respects as being primarily symbolic. I will close with my perspective on the next step in the legal controversy over vouchers.

The Holding

In *Zelman*, the Court highlighted two factors as being crucial to its holding that vouchers for private religious schools do not contravene the Establishment Clause: program neutrality and private choice. First, the Court held that eligibility under the scholarship program, both as to participating schools and student eligibility, was religiously neutral, meaning that the program neither favored religion nor created incentives for religious use.[3] Examining the *face* of the statute (rather than its application), the Court emphasized that the scholarship is part of general undertaking to provide educational services, that it confers its benefit to a broad class of individuals without reference to religion, and that it permits participation of all schools within the Cleveland and adjoining school districts, public and private alike. As Chief Justice Rehnquist wrote: "government programs that neutrally provide benefits to a broad class of citizens defined without reference to religion are not readily subject to an Establishment Clause challenge."[4]

3. Id. at 2467–68.
4. Id. at 2467.

Second, the Court emphasized the element of *private choice*, finding that the public aid reaches religious schools "only as a result of genuine and independent choices of private individuals."[5] "Where a government aid program . . . provides assistance directly to a broad class of citizens who, in turn, direct government aid to religious schools wholly as a result of their own genuine and independent private choice, the program is not readily subject to challenge under the Establishment Clause."[6]

The Court's reliance on neutrality as the organizing paradigm for Establishment Clause cases is troubling. As I have discussed elsewhere, neutrality is insufficient as a constitutional value because it (1) lacks any independent, substantive meaning and (2) obscures other Establishment Clause values central to our constitutional system.[7] Neutrality is not self-defining; it must draw its substance from other sources.[8] As Justice Souter demonstrated in his *Mitchell v. Helms* dissent, the Court has used the term "neutrality" to represent quite disparate concepts: secular or nonreligious; a median between religious and secular; and evenhanded treatment.[9] Even if neutrality is equated with evenhandedness, as is advocated by a Court plurality and Kenneth Starr, it is an inadequate proxy for the "spacious conception" of religious freedom found in

5. Id. at 2466.

6. Id. at 2467.

7. See Steven K. Green, "Of (Un)Equal Jurisprudential Pedigree: Rectifying the Imbalance Between Neutrality and Separationism," 43 B.C. L. Rev. 1111, 1131–33 (September 2002); Steven K. Green, "The Ambiguity of Neutrality," 86 Cornell L. Rev. 692, 706–08 (March 2001).

8. See Douglas Laycock, "Formal, Substantive, and Disaggregated Neutrality Toward Religion," 39 DePaul L. Rev. 993, 998 (Summer 1990) ("We must specify the content of neutrality by looking to other principles in the religion clauses").

9. See *Mitchell v. Helms*, 530 U.S. 793, 878–84 (2000) (Souter, J., dissenting).

the Establishment Clause.[10] The Court's version of formal, evenhanded neutrality is concerned only with *equal treatment* of participants and is divorced from substantive considerations of starting and ending points. The Court's version also lacks regard for the comprehensiveness of treatment, which should be central to notions of equality. No voucher program will ever assist more than a minuscule number of students or provide a comprehensive solution to the problem of "failing schools." Finally, evenhanded neutrality is incomplete as a constitutional doctrine because it fails to account for other important values that inform the religion clauses, such as protecting religious liberty and autonomy, ensuring interreligious equality, alleviating religious dissension, and protecting the legitimacy and integrity of government and religion.[11]

In a similar manner, reliance on "private choice" obscures larger considerations of the degree and comprehensiveness of government subsidies of religion, concerns that lie at the heart of the nonestablishment mandate.[12] As discussed below, voucher aid can involve substantial transfers of public funds to religion, create dependency on the government largesse, and threaten the autonomy and integrity of religious institutions. These concerns arise irrespective of whether the act of private choice is truly genuine, meaningful, and independent.

Granted, we acknowledged in our brief that private choice *could* be a factor in assessing an Establishment Clause viola-

10. See *McCollum v. Bd. of Educ.*, 333 U.S. 203, 213 (1948) (Frankfurter, J., concurring).

11. See Green, "Of (Un)Equal Jurisprudential Pedigree," 43 B.C. L. Rev. at 1131–33.

12. See: Steven K. Green, "Private School Vouchers and the Confusion Over 'Direct' Aid," 10 Geo. Mason Univ. Civ. R. L. J. 47 (Winter 1999/Spring 2000); Laura S. Underkuffler, "Vouchers and Beyond: The Individual as Causative Agent in Establishment Clause Jurisprudence," 75 Ind. L. J. 167 (Winter 2000).

tion—that "true private choice," as Justice O'Connor termed it two years earlier[13]—could neutralize the constitutional infirmity of aid advancing religion, but only where a broad universe of options exists among which to choose. Choice is only genuine and meaningful if the beneficiary has a wide variety of options, exercises some independent control over the funds, and is not effectively forced to redeem his benefit only at religious sources. Otherwise, the beneficiary's control and discretion over how the funds are applied would be transparent, and the ultimate use at a religious school would correctly be attributable to the state.[14]

We pointed to the fact that over 80 percent of schools participating under the Cleveland program are religious and that when one considered the number of seats available to voucher-eligible students, the ratio rises to 96 percent religious. (Actually, during the 2001–2002 school year, religious seats accounted for 99 percent of the available private school openings). We also noted that no suburban public school participates in the program, nor are any likely to participate based on past practice under both the voucher program and interdistrict transfer programs. This means that meaningful choice is illusive; that if you are a parent with a voucher, 99 percent of the potential uses are at religious schools. This skewing of options creates an incentive for religious education and is unconstitutional.

The Court rejected our argument that "true private choice" does not exist, despite the preponderance of religious schools participating under the program. Initially, the majority reiter-

13. *Mitchell v. Helms*, 530 U.S. 793, 842 (2000) (O'Connor, J., concurring in the judgment).
14. See *Zobrest v. Catalina Foothills Sch. Dist.*, 509 U.S. 1, 10 (1993) (noting that as a prerequisite for constitutionality, beneficiary choices "cannot be attributed to state decisionmaking").

ated that the number of students who end up in religious schools under the program is irrelevant. Provided the program is neutral on its face, the amount of government aid channeled to religious institutions by recipients has no constitutional significance—that it would be loath to have a constitutional rule turn on how program beneficiaries choose to exercise their options.[15]

This part of the ruling mischaracterized our argument (and sidestepped the issue of neutrality) in two respects. First, we argued that the 99 percent figure is indicative not of how parents have decided to exercise their options in a truly open universe *but of the availability of options themselves.* As stated, in Cleveland, if a parent wants her child to participate in the voucher program, there is a mathematical certainty that she will attend a religious school, regardless of what that parent desires.[16] This makes the ultimate placement decision attributable to the state. Second, we argued that the Court could not presume the neutrality of the program merely from its face but rather from how it works in practice. The fact that 99 percent of options are religious indicates that the program is not truly neutral, notwithstanding the absence of any religious language in the statute. Neutrality cannot be determined in isolation of the facts.

The Court also held (primarily through Justice O'Connor) that the appropriate universe to consider for genuine private choice is not that of the participating private schools but includes magnet, charter, and possibly even public schools.[17]

---

15. 122 S. Ct. at 2470.

16. Id. at 2496 (Souter, J., dissenting) ("The 96.6 percent reflects, instead, the fact that too few nonreligious school desks are available and few but religious schools can afford to accept more than a handful of voucher students").

17. Id. at 2469, 2478.

The Court maintained that voucher parents are able to consider all of these educational options for their children (even though some magnet and charter schools do not offer the same grades as the religious schools), and when one considers all these alternatives, the percentage of children attending religious schools drops to under 20 percent.[18] The fact that two nonreligious private schools had converted to community/charter schools after the program was initiated added credence to the argument that the various types of schools are all part of the same universe of options for the parents.

Despite that last fact, the Court still chose the wrong baseline, for the entire purpose of the voucher program is to provide an *alternative* to public schooling. If a parent desires a voucher in order to remove his child from the public schools, considering those options in the universe—or at least traditional public school offerings in the mix[19]—is analytically dishonest and skews the range of true *alternatives* for parents. For those parents, the alternative of the public schools is already closed.

Second, eligibility for the various educational alternatives often varies widely, as do program content and emphasis. Some programs are needs-based, some are competitive, others rely on lotteries for entry, while all options are affected by factors such as convenience, available transportation, and program content. For example, a magnet school with a French immersion program or one for math-gifted students may not be a realistic option for many children. Although a small number of children may be eligible for several of the education alternatives, most children will likely qualify for only one alternative. Justice O'Connor resorted to a high degree of formalism

18. Id. at 2471.
19. Id. at 2469 ("schoolchildren enjoy a range of options: They may remain in public school").

by claiming that a community/charter school does not have to offer the same grades or programs as a religious school to represent an option for a voucher-eligible student.[20]

Third, there is a qualitative difference between public and private schools that argues against including public schools in the constitutional equation. Differences in funding schemes, accountability requirements, curriculum standards, and legal obligations distinguish the two institutions. This consideration leads to a fourth: even if charter and magnet schools should be included within the greater universe of options, that consideration fails to address the composition of the *private school* universe. For parents who prefer a private school alternative, there should be a balanced secular-sectarian mix to guarantee that choice is not skewed. A state cannot circumvent its constitutional obligation of nonadvancement of religion by creating a predominately religious program but then seeking to counterbalance it with two or three secular programs. The constitutionality of each program must stand in its own. Otherwise, the no-funding prohibition would lose all meaning, since the state could always point to other related programs to counteract the purposeful support of religion.[21]

The Court's discussion of the appropriate universe of options, however, represents a less than clear victory for voucher proponents. Its emphasis on the availability of magnet and charter schools alternatives indicates that a state must provide a broad array of secular education options to ensure the constitutionality of a voucher program. One could argue that under the holding, secular options must predominate—that the Court's 20 percent religious figure sets a benchmark. Also,

---

20. Id. at 2479.

21. See id. at 2493 (Souter, J., dissenting). See Steven K. Green, "The Illusionary Aspect of 'Private Choice' for Constitutional Analysis," 38 Willamette L. Rev. 549, 571–72 (Fall 2002).

there is O'Connor's interesting comment that nonreligious school alternatives need not be *superior* to religious schools to be an option, but that they must be *adequate.*[22] This suggests that a state could not offer a religiously dominated voucher program as the only alternative to a failing public school system without the existence of charter and magnet schools. These interpretations stand in contrast, however, to the Court's formalistic approach that focuses on the facial neutrality of the program, an approach that is willing to look outside the contours of a particular program to consider related educational opportunities.

The Significance of *Zelman*

The question of whether *Zelman* was correctly decided does not address the issue of its significance. Is *Zelman* a watershed ruling, a seminal holding? Does it constitute a change in the jurisprudence, and what are its implications for future litigation? Or, to the contrary, does *Zelman* represent merely the natural culmination of the Court's evolving jurisprudence, such that the holding is primarily symbolic?

Few Establishment Clause cases had been as eagerly anticipated or received as much build-up as *Zelman.* Prior to the decision, *Church & State* magazine called *Zelman* "the most important education funding case in 50 years," and Dean John Jeffries of University of Virginia Law School characterized the holding as presenting "the most important church-state issue of our time."[23] More than 100 groups weighed in with amicus briefs, with both sides predicting dire consequences for the

22. 122 S. Ct. at 2477 (O'Connor, J., concurring).
23. *Church & State* (November 2001); John C. Jeffries Jr., and James E. Ryan, "A Political History of the Establishment Clause," 100 Mich. L. Rev. 279 (November 2001).

Constitution and education policy from an unfavorable decision.

In contrast to the advance billing, the Court majority and Justice O'Connor played down the significance of their holding. Both opinions sought to put the decision within the mainstream of Establishment Clause jurisprudence, or at least within the developments over the past twenty years. Chief Justice Rehnquist wrote that the decision fit squarely within a jurisprudence of "true private choice programs [that] has remained consistent and unbroken."[24] Justice O'Connor was more adamant, asserting that the holding did not, "when considered in light of other longstanding government programs that impact religious organizations and our prior Establishment Clause jurisprudence, mark a dramatic break from the past."[25] Later in her concurrence, as if to persuade an unconvinced audience, O'Connor reiterated that "today's decision [does not] signal a major departure from this Court's prior Establishment Clause jurisprudence."[26]

On one level, O'Connor is correct: the decision does not effect a major change in the law. The Court has been speaking about neutral programs of general applicability for over fifty years[27] and of independent choice for close to twenty years.[28] It placed its holding squarely within the earlier decisions of *Mueller v. Allen, Witters v. Washington Department of Services for the Blind, Zobrest v. Catalina Foothills School District, Agostini v. Felton*, and *Mitchell v. Helms* that discussed indirect aid.[29] These decisions, Rehnquist wrote, "have drawn a

---

24. 122 S. Ct. at 2467, 2466.
25. Id. at 2473 (O'Connor, J., concurring).
26. Id. at 2476.
27. See *Everson v. Board of Education*, 330 U.S. 1, 16–17 (1947).
28. See *Mueller v. Allen*, 463 U.S. 388, 399 (1983).
29. 122 S. Ct. at 2465–68.

consistent distinction between government aid programs that provide aid directly to religious schools . . . and programs of true private choice."[30] In relying on these holdings, *Zelman* added little new to the law. More significantly, the *Zelman* holding does not disturb the distinction between direct and indirect government aid to religious institutions, the former form being prohibited. Neither *Zelman* nor those earlier hold-ings apply to "programs that provide aid *directly* [from the gov-ernment] to religious schools," Rehnquist noted.[31] Thus, a state could not allocate direct aid to private schools on a per capita basis.

Zelman is thus a cautious decision; it broke no new legal ground and declined to reverse any earlier holdings, preferring to distinguish decisions to the contrary.[32] In fact, Rehnquist reaffirmed that the appropriate standard of review remains the much maligned *Lemon* test, which asks whether a state law has the purpose or effect of advancing or inhibiting religion.[33] O'Connor echoed that the "test today is basically the same as that set forth in [the 1963 school prayer cases]."[34] Of course, this is the Court's job, to legitimate its decisions by relying on precedent and stare decisis.

Considering only the law, one could argue that *Zelman* is a jurisprudential step *back* from two years earlier. In *Mitchell v. Helms*, the Court upheld the direct grant of Chapter 2 mate-rials—library books, equipment, computers—to religious schools. There, the plurality emphasized the neutrality of the Chapter 2 program, suggesting that was all that was necessary

30. Id. at 2465.

31. Id.

32. Id. at 2472 (distinguishing *Committee for Public Education v. Nyquist*, 413 U.S. 756 (1973)).

33. Id. at 2465. See *Lemon v. Kurtzman*, 403 U.S. 602, 612–13 (1971).

34. 122 S. Ct. at 2476 (O'Connor, J., concurring).

for constitutionality. Provided government acted evenhand-edly, it could fund all aspects of religious education.[35] Although private choice might help ensure the constitution-ality of a program, it was not a necessary ingredient.[36] That holding brought a strong rebuke from O'Connor, who called the plurality's sole emphasis on neutrality a "rule of unprec-edented breadth."[37] As a result, in order to secure O'Connor's vote, the *Zelman* decision emphasizes the private choice aspect of vouchers and does not hang its hat on program neu-trality. Thus, for the purposes of doctrinal development, *Zel-man* is much more symbolic than it is a seminal decision.

The fact that *Zelman* may not represent a watershed in Establishment Clause jurisprudence does not mean that it is without significance. Although the majority applied existing law, the decision signifies the dominance of neutrality and pri-vate choice theories in the government benefits side of Estab-lishment Clause jurisprudence. As discussed above, the Court's increasing reliance on neutrality, to the exclusion of separationist principles, is troubling because it ignores other religion clause values that are "of equal historical and juris-prudential pedigree."[38] Even if neutrality is the correct analyt-ical standard for judging such controversies, the majority misapplied the law by finding neutrality and private choice in a case where neither principle existed. And finally, *Zelman* must be considered significant if for no other reason than it answers that nagging "voucher question." With the exception of integration and school prayer, few education issues have

35. *Mitchell*, 530 U.S. at 809–10.

36. Id. at 816 ("Although the presence of private choice is easier to see when aid literally passes through the hands of individuals . . . there is no reason why the Establishment Clause requires such a form").

37. Id. at 837 (O'Connor, J., concurring in the judgment)

38. *Rosenberger v. Rector and Visitors of the University of Virginia*, 515 U.S. 819, 849 (1995) (O'Connor, J., concurring).

been as contentious. Although possibly not seminal for breaking new legal ground, *Zelman* is highly significant for what it has wrought.

First, the holding opens the door to substantial transfers of public funds to religious schools. Under the Milwaukee and Cleveland programs alone, the annual amount of public funding flowing to private schools is $40 and $8 million, respectively.[39] The Court claimed that substantiality on its own has never been a concern, particularly in choice situations,[40] but O'Connor spent several pages contrasting the amount of the voucher aid to other funding and tax breaks that already flow to religious institutions so as to demonstrate its comparative insignificance.[41] Possibly, she protests too much. *Zelman* authorizes statewide voucher programs, such as in Florida, which, if fully implemented, could result in billions of unrestricted dollars flowing to religious schools.

Substantially also means more than the gross amounts, which will always pale when compared with the billions of dollars spent on public education. Under prior holdings, aid is also considered substantial if it subsidizes the religious educational mission or pays for the entire educational experience of children attending religious schools.[42] Previously, permissible aid was in discrete and focused forms (for example, Title I programs) that supplemented the private schools' costs but

---

39. See U.S. General Accounting Office, *School Vouchers: Publicly Funded Programs in Cleveland and Milwaukee* (August 2001).

40. 122 S. Ct. at 2466, 2470. But see *Witters*, 474 U.S. at 488 (noting that "[no] significant portion of the aid expended under the Washington program as a whole will end up flowing to religious education").

41. Id. at 2473–76 (O'Connor, J., concurring).

42. *Zobrest*, 509 U.S. at 12 (discussing "substantial" aid); *Grand Rapids School District v. Ball*, 473 U.S. 373, 394 (1985) (same); *Meek v. Pittenger*, 431 U.S. 349, 365 (1975) (discussing the prohibition on "massive aid").

did not supplant their educational obligations.[43] Also, the Court often noted that no public funds flowed to the coffers of religious schools.[44] After *Zelman*, a state may pay the entire educational costs of a student to attend a religious school. And apparently, there is nothing to prevent a religious school from being composed entirely of voucher students. This is *substantial* aid, any way you slice it.

Finally, *Zelman* is significant in that it authorizes payment for religious instruction and worship. Under previous aid decisions, the Court emphasized that the government aid was secular and could not be applied to religious uses.[45] This prior barrier, however, is now broken under the aegis of private choice. Even Justice O'Connor acknowledged that *Zelman* is distinct from other indirect aid cases because a significant portion of the funds reaches religious schools without restrictions on their use.[46] Justice Souter is correct that issues of substantiality and divertability had long been central to Establishment Clause jurisprudence.[47] Now they are not.

The Future for Vouchers

What, then, is the next step in the legal battle over vouchers? Clearly, *Zelman* does not obligate states to establish voucher programs, but holds only that it is constitutional to create programs that include religious schools. The most immediate issue on the horizon concerns the ability of states to operate educational funding and scholarship programs that exclude

---

43. *Agostini*, 521 U.S. at 228.

44. Id.; *Zobrest*, 509 U.S. at 10.

45. *Agostini*, 521 U.S. at 223, 228; *Zobrest*, 509 U.S. at 10; *Bowen v. Kendrick*, 487 U.S. 589, 611–12 (1988); *Sloan v. Lemon*, 413 U.S. 825, 829 (1973).

46. 122 S. Ct. at 2473 (O'Connor, J., concurring).

47. Id. at 2490 (Souter, J., dissenting).

religious schools or prohibit the use of the scholarships in religious programs.[48]

One example is found in programs that are unique to Maine and Vermont that permit towns without public schools to tuition-out their students to neighboring public and private schools. Both states prohibit using the tuition grants at religious schools. During the mid-1990s, three cases were litigated in Maine and Vermont over these restrictive grants, the issue being whether the exclusion of religious schools discriminated against religion in violation of the free exercise, free speech, and equal protection clauses.[49] In all cases courts upheld the exclusion, but those holdings turned primarily on the fact that the Establishment Clause required such distinctive treatment.[50] With *Zelman*, that compelling government interest in avoiding an Establishment Clause violation apparently vanishes. As a result, the Institute for Justice has recently filed a new action in Maine asserting that the disparate treatment under state tuitioning violates Equal Protection.[51]

The second example is those state college scholarship programs that prohibit the use of state aid at either pervasively sectarian colleges or in programs of religious study.[52] As in the Maine and Vermont cases, many of these statutes are based on distinct state constitutional provisions that often require a

48. A second important issue, outside the scope of this conference, concerns the ability of states to impose conditions on recipient religious schools—such as curriculum and nondiscrimination requirements—that may threaten the schools' religious autonomy interests.

49. See *Strout v. Albanese*, 178 F.3d 57 (1st Cir. 1999); *Bagley v. Raymond School District*, 728 A.2d 127 (Me. 1999); *Chittenden Town School District v. Dept. of Educ.*, 738 A.2d 539 (Vt. 1999).

50. See *Strout*, 178 F.3d at 60–62.

51. See *Anderson v. Town of Durham*, Cumberland County (Me.), Superior Court.

52. See, e.g., *Columbia Union College v. Clarke*, 159 F.3d 151 (4th Cir. 1998).

more rigorous separation between church and state. Approximately thirty-five states have constitutional provisions that explicitly bar funds flowing to religious institutions.[53] An example is Article I, section 6, of the Indiana constitution, which states that "[n]o money shall be drawn from the treasury for the benefit of any religious or theological institution." Article 8, section 3, adds that "[t]he principal of the Common School fund shall remain a perpetual fund . . . and the income thereof shall be inviolably appropriated to the support of Common Schools, and to no other purpose whatsoever." In common parlance, these provisions are often called "Blaine amendments," or "Baby-Blaines," in that many are based on a failed attempt in 1876 to amend the U.S. Constitution to prohibit public funding of parochial schools.[54]

The question presented by these stricter state constitutional provisions is whether they can serve as free-standing constitutional justifications for distinguishing between religious and nonreligious recipients, or whether they must give way to the federal equal protection and free exercise interests. Not more than two months following *Zelman*, a state trial court struck down Florida's voucher program based on the state constitution which provides that "[n]o revenue from the state or any political subdivision or agency thereof shall ever be taken from the public treasury, directly or indirectly in aid of any church, sect, or religious denomination or in aid of any sectarian institution."[55] The Florida appellate courts will be

---

53. See Note, "School Choice and State Constitutions," 86 Va. L. Rev. 117, 123 (2000).

54. See Steven K. Green, "The Blaine Amendment Reconsidered," 36 Am. J. Legal Hist. 38 (1992).

55. *Holmes v. Bush*, Case No. CV 99-3370 (Aug. 5, 2002); Fla. Const. Art. I § 3.

forced to reconcile this constitutional provision with the intervenors' free exercise and equal protection claims.

More recently, in a case called *Davey v. Locke*, the Ninth Circuit held that Washington State's refusal to allow an otherwise eligible student to use a state scholarship for a ministerial program violated the free exercise clause, notwithstanding the stricter command of the Washington constitution.[56] The court held that the prohibition on using the scholarship for ministerial training discriminated on the basis of religion, such that the state constitution had to give way. This holding conflicts with an earlier Ninth Circuit decision that such denials violate neither equal protection nor free exercise—that the state is merely exercising its authority to fund those programs it chooses, and that no one can demand that the government subsidize expression of a constitutional right.[57] The Supreme Court has granted review in *Davey*, potentially to resolve this conflict between stricter state constitutions and federally guaranteed rights, although the Court could also find the free exercise claim is insufficient.

Admittedly, this presents a close issue. On the one hand, state courts may interpret their constitutions to afford greater protection than guaranteed under the federal constitution.[58] The assumption has been that states can provide a more rigorous separation of church and state just as they can provide greater protection against search and seizure. Also, the government may selectively fund certain programs without being required to fund related programs and without succumbing to viewpoint discrimination.[59] The decisions upholding limita-

56. *Davey v. Locke*, 299 F.3d 748 (9th Cir. 2002); cert. granted 123 S. Ct. 2075 (2003).
57. *KDM v. Reedsport Sch. Dist.*, 196 F.3d 1046 (9th Cir. 1999).
58. See *Pruneyard Shopping Center v. Robins*, 447 U.S. 74 (1980).
59. See *Rosenberger*, 515 U.S. at 833.

tions on funding of abortion-related services affirm this rule.[60] As the Court has indicated on several occasions:

> [Government] may selectively fund a program to encourage certain activities it believes to be in the public interest, without at the same time funding an alternative program in another way . . . In doing so, the Government has not discriminated on the basis of viewpoint; it has merely chosen to fund one activity to the exclusion of the other."[61]

Finally, earlier Court holdings indicate that states do not violate equal protection by refusing to fund private education.[62]

On the other hand, some states have already decided to fund private schooling but are excluding private religious schooling only. This is a distinction based on religion and implicates free speech, free exercise, and equal protection values. The argument is that while states are under no obligation to fund private education, once they do so, they cannot make eligibility turn on religious affiliation.[63] However, in *Rust v. Sullivan*, the government was also funding only one side of the debate—family counseling that discouraged abortion—but the Court found no viewpoint discrimination.[64]

The outcome will likely turn on how broadly or narrowly courts define these values and view the distinctive treatment. In the *Davey* case, the distinctive treatment was not directed against any group of persons (and Mr. Davey was not a member of a protected class), but against the use of a state benefit. Washington State did not declare Mr. Davey ineligible based

60. See *Harris v. McRae*, 448 U.S. 297 (1980); *Maher v. Roe*, 432 U.S. 464 (1977).

61. *NEA v. Finley*, 524 U.S. 569, 588 (1999) (quoting *Rust v. Sullivan*, 500 U.S. 173, 193 (1991)).

62. *Norwood v. Harrison*, 413 U.S. 455, 462 (1973).

63. *Davey*, 299 F.3d at 756.

64. 500 U.S. at 193–94 (not singling out a disfavored group on basis of speech).

on his religion, but merely placed limits on how he could use the state scholarship. Mr. Davey, irrespective of whether he is an evangelical or not, could still receive a scholarship to attend a state university and could even apply it at his religious college, just not toward a program of religious training.[65]

Still, because the state is funding other types of degree programs it appears to be denying a benefit on the basis of religion. The question may turn on whether the state has created a funded forum for diverse educational perspectives and is discriminating on the basis of religious viewpoints. The closer the analogy to a speech-related forum, the stronger the argument that the state cannot distinguish between applications or perspectives.[66]

Such cases may also turn on how courts view the purpose behind the Blaine amendments. Some people are seeking to tar the Blaine amendments with religious animus—particularly, anti-Catholicism—to show that the purpose of such state provisions is to discriminate against religion.[67] If that can be proved, then the states' reliance on the state constitutions may be invalid. To be sure, some of the impetus for the Blaine amendments rested on nativism and anti-Catholicism—to keep parochial schools from receiving public funding.[68] Without a doubt, nineteenth-century nativist groups such as the American Protective Association used the Blaine amendments to further their bigoted cause.

Focusing solely on this aspect obscures the much larger dynamic at work 150 years ago, when public schools were still

65. *Davey*, 299 F.3d at 761 (McKeown, J., dissenting).

66. Contrast *Rosenberger*, 515 U.S. at 837 (forum analysis applies), with *Finley*, 524 U.S. at 586 (rejecting forum analysis).

67. See the Web site for the Becket Fund for Religious Liberty, *www.blaineamendments.org/*.

68. See Green, n. 44 above.

in their infancy and faced significant hurdles of funding, public acceptability, and hostility to universal education. Free, universal, and nonsectarian public education was still a novel idea, and the mere fact that officials viewed funding of private religious schools as a threat to that ideal does not necessarily translate into religious animus. Not only Catholics but Lutheran, Baptist, Methodist, and Presbyterian schools desired public funding.[69] Public schools were seen as the engine of democracy and equality while private schooling was exclusive and class-reinforcing. The no-funding rule thus ensured the survival of public schooling and furthered ideals of equality and inclusion. The mere fact that state constitutions exclude funding of religious education does not mean they have or had the purpose or object of suppressing religion or religious conduct. Irrespective of the motives of some constitution drafters, public funding of religious instruction and worship strikes at the heart of Establishment Clause values. Lest we forget, nonestablishment is also a means of ensuring religious liberty.

This controversy over state constitutional prohibitions thus represents the next legal battleground for vouchers. It is likely the Supreme Court will have to resolve this issue, too. With *Davey* already before the Court, we may have an answer to this question sooner than later. But if the past is any guide, this uncertainty may continue for several years.

69. William Oland Bourne, *History of the Public School Society of the City of New York* (New York: William Wood & Co., 1870), pp. 48–75; Diane Ravitch, *The Great School Wars* (New York: Basic Books, 1974), p. 40.

3

Sunshine Replaces the Cloud

CLINT BOLICK

The June 27, 2002, decision of the United States Supreme Court in *Zelman v. Simmons-Harris*[1] is the most important education decision since *Brown v. Board of Education*,[2] for it opens an array of policy options by which to address the urgent crisis of urban education. Equally important, the 5–4 decision provides jurisprudential support for the right of parents to direct and control the nature of their children's education.

The reaction among opponents of school choice[3] to the decision was predictably histrionic. The ill-named National Education Association and People for the American Way pro-

This paper is adapted from a forthcoming article that will appear in the first issue of the *Cato Supreme Court Review*.

1. 122 S. Ct. 2460 (2002).
2. 347 U.S. 483 (1954).
3. "School choice" can have a variety of meanings, but I use it to encompass publicly supported private school options, whether through vouchers or tax credits for tuition or scholarships. I support deregulated public "charter" schools, but believe that choice is not meaningful (or optimally effective in its competitive effects) if it is constrained to the public sector. For a broader explication of the imperative of school choice, see Clint Bolick, *Transformation: The Promise and Politics of Empowerment* (Oakland, Calif.: Institute for Contemporary Studies, 1998), pp. 43–53.

nounced the opinion a disaster for public education. Barry Lynn of Americans United for Separation of Church and State characterized the decision as a "wrecking ball" for the First Amendment's prohibition of religious establishment. The Court's dissenters agreed, predicting all manner of religious strife.

On the contrary, the decision marks no significant jurisprudential innovation, for as the Court observes, it fits neatly within "an unbroken line of decisions rejecting challenges to similar programs."[4] But its real-world impact is potentially titanic. That is because the case is really not about religion at all, but rather about the distribution of power over education. And that is why the main challengers are not advocates of separation of church and state, but teachers unions, who otherwise couldn't care less about religious establishment. In the end, the Court recognized that the "primary effect" of the Cleveland Scholarship Program was not to advance religion but to expand educational opportunities, and appropriately concluded that allowing parents to direct a portion of public education funds to the schools of their choice, public or private, does not constitute religious establishment. What is far more surprising than the outcome is that four justices could disagree.[5]

Much as school integration did not instantly appear after *Brown*, so too will school choice not immediately materialize after *Zelman*. Serious legal obstacles remain in the form of state

4. *Zelman*, 122 S. Ct. at 2473.
5. Illustrating that the academic consensus is broad that school choice is constitutional was an amicus curiae brief prepared by former Berkeley law school dean Jesse Choper on behalf of three dozen law professors reflecting a broad philosophical spectrum. In addition to the professors signing the brief, prominent liberal academics taking the same view include Laurence Tribe, Douglas Laycock, Jeffrey Rosen, Samuel Estraicher, Akhil Amar, and former U.S. Solicitor General Walter Dellinger.

constitutional provisions that are more explicit with regard to separation of church and state than the federal constitution. And school choice advocates still face powerful special-interest opposition in legislative arenas. But the Supreme Court has made it clear that there are no federal constitutional impediments; and it may yet again play an important role in removing discriminatory state constitutional barriers that stand in the path of expanding educational opportunities for children who need them desperately.

The Omnipresent Cloud

For as long as school choice has appeared on the policy horizon, constitutional questions have dogged it. Every school choice program adopted before 2000—whether vouchers or tax credits—was promptly subjected to legal challenge. The teachers unions brought out federal Establishment Clause (or, as they call it, "separation of church and state")[6] claims as well as state analogs, along with whatever other state constitutional claims they could pull out of their bag of tricks. Moreover, as we pointed out in our petition for writ of *certiorari* in the U.S. Supreme Court, constitutional objections repeatedly have been raised against school choice proposals in the legislative context. So it was imperative for school choice proponents to remove this major obstacle to reform. Dating from the enactment of the first urban school choice program in Milwaukee in 1990, the task took a dozen years.

Before and during that time, the Supreme Court considered a number of cases dealing with various types of programs in which aid found its way into religious institutions. Two seem-

6. The First Amendment provides in relevant part that "Congress shall make no law respecting an establishment of religion, or prohibiting the free exercise thereof."

ingly irreconcilable sets of precedents emerged. The first, reflecting a long period in which the Court's jurisprudence demanded a rigorous separation of church and state and evidenced a hostility toward religion, culminated in *Committee for Public Education v. Nyquist*, a 1973 decision striking down a package of religious school aid programs.[7] The second, emanating from the view that the religion clauses of the First Amendment require governmental "neutrality" toward religion, produced six consecutive decisions sustaining direct and indirect aid programs.[8] The apparently disparate frameworks resulted in divergent decisions among lower courts over school choice. Courts that found *Nyquist* controlling invariably found school choice programs unconstitutional; courts that found the subsequent cases controlling upheld them.

In fact, the two sets of precedents are harmonious. In *Nyquist*, the state provided loans, tax deductions, and other support exclusively for private schools and students who patronized them. The program was aimed at bailing out religious schools that were closing, and whose students were returning to public schools at considerable taxpayer expense. Applying the three-part Establishment Clause framework first set forth in *Lemon v. Kurtzman*, 403 U.S. 602 (1973),[9] the Court concluded that the program's "primary effect" was to advance religion. The reasons for the Court's decision were understandable. Though acknowledging the strong secular purpose of pro-

---

7. 413 U.S. 756 (1973).

8. *Mueller v. Allen*, 463 U.S. 388 (1983); *Witters v. Wash. Dept. of Services for the Blind*, 474 U.S. 481 (1986); *Zobrest v. Catalina Foothills School Dist.*, 509 U.S. 1 (1993); *Rosenberger v. Rector and Visitors of the Univ. of Va.*, 515 U.S. 819 (1995); *Agostini v. Felton*, 521 U.S. 203 (1997); *Mitchell v. Helms*, 530 U.S. 793 (2000).

9. In assessing aid programs, the Court assessed whether the program (1) has a secular purpose, (2) has a primary effect that neither advances nor inhibits religion, and (3) excessively entangles the state and religion.

viding educational opportunities outside the public educational sector, the Court looked at the aid programs and found that they were skewed entirely in favor of private schools. And among private schools, religious schools heavily predominated. Because the program was not "neutral" in that it defined its beneficiaries in terms of the (private) schools they attended, and because the beneficiaries by definition over-whelmingly attended religious schools, the Court held that the aid scheme had the impermissible primary effect of advancing religion. Given that it was the program's aim to help religious schools and their patrons, the decision was not surprising.

Had *Nyquist* been more categorical in its repudiation of school choice—adopting the separationists' position that the moment a dollar of public funds crosses the threshold of a religious school that it is unconstitutional—it would have destroyed any chance for school choice programs. Fortunately, the Court created an escape valve. It probably did so because it recognized that the door to such aid already had been opened through such enormously popular programs as the G.I. Bill and Pell Grants. So in a footnote, the Court planted the seeds of an exception, one that eventually would become the general rule to which *Nyquist* would become the exception. Specifically, the Court held open the question of "whether the significantly religious character of the statute's beneficiaries might differ-entiate the present cases from a case involving some form of public assistance (for example, scholarships) made available generally without regard to the sectarian-nonsectarian, or pub-lic-nonpublic nature of the institution benefited."[10]

The Court returned to that question for the first time a decade later in *Mueller*. There the Court examined a Minnesota tax deduction for educational expenses. Because public school

10. *Nyquist*, 413 U.S. at 782 n. 38.

parents incur few expenses, the vast majority of tax deductions—allegedly 96 percent—were claimed by private school parents. The facts seemed eerily like those presented in *Nyquist*. But by a 5–4 vote, the Court upheld the deductions in a decision written by then–Associate Justice William Rehnquist and, notably, joined by Justice Powell, who had written *Nyquist*. The Court distinguished *Nyquist* on two main grounds: (1) all of the money that flowed to religious schools through tax deductions did so only as a result of independent choices made by families; (2) the program was neutral on its face, extending benefits to public and private school parents alike. The Court rejected the invitation to apply some sort of mathematical formula regarding the percentage of the program's beneficiaries attending religious schools in order to determine the program's primary effect. "We would be loath to adopt a rule grounding the constitutionality of a facially neutral law on annual reports reciting the extent to which various classes of private citizens claimed benefits under the law," the Court declared.[11] Departing from a rule of facial neutrality, the Court emphasized, would render the constitutional inquiry hopelessly subjective. "Such an approach would scarcely provide the certainty that this field stands in need of," the Court explained, "nor can we perceive principled standards by which such statistical evidence might be evaluated."[12] Ultimately, the Court concluded that "[t]he historic purposes of the [Establishment] Clause simply do not encompass the sort of attenuated financial benefit, ultimately controlled by the private choices of individual parents, that eventually flows to parochial schools from the neutrally available tax benefit at issue in this case."[13]

11. *Mueller*, 463 U.S. at 401.
12. Id.
13. Id. at 400.

Jurisprudentially, the battle over school choice was over once *Mueller* was decided—a fact that the dissenters in *Zelman* nearly two decades later explicitly would acknowledge. *Mueller* provided the framework that would henceforth consistently apply, holding that aid that found its way into religious schools was constitutionally permissible so long as two criteria were present: (1) the aid was directed to religious institutions only as a result of the independent decisions of parents and students ("indirect aid"), and (2) religious entities were only one of the options available ("neutrality"). That framework was entirely congenial to school choice programs, whether vouchers or tax credits, and school choice advocates now had a constitutional road map by which to craft programs.

Mueller also disposed of a troublesome argument, articulated by the Court in prior cases, that college aid programs were conceptually different from elementary and secondary school programs, because children in elementary and secondary schools are more impressionable and therefore more susceptible to religious school indoctrination. Though *Mueller* did not address the question directly, it was implicitly subsumed within the concept of parental choice. In cases involving public schools, such as school prayer cases, a doctrine of relative impressionability seems appropriate. But in indirect aid cases, children are hearing a religious message only because of their parents' choice. In essence, parental choice operates as a constitutional "circuit breaker" between church and state.

Mueller also would impact *Zelman* in its rejection of a mathematical formula for determining Establishment Clause violations. The most troublesome fact in the record of the Cleveland program was that the overwhelming majority of students receiving scholarships were attending religious schools. *Mueller* confronted that issue head-on, subsuming it within both prongs of the inquiry, facial neutrality and indirect aid, and established a firm rule basing a program's constitutionality on facial neutrality.

The Court reinforced those criteria three years later in *Witters*, which involved the use of college aid by a blind student studying for the ministry in a school of divinity. It is hard to imagine an atmosphere more pervasively sectarian than that; yet the Court upheld the use of the aid in a unanimous decision by Justice Thurgood Marshall.[14] The Court emphasized that few students likely would use the aid in religious schools or for religious vocations. In *Zelman*, anti–school choice advocates seized upon that language to suggest that religious schools appropriately could comprise only a small part of a broader aid program.

But writing separate concurring opinions, five justices reiterated the more expansive criteria set forth in *Mueller*. Most notably, Justice Powell articulated a clear neutrality standard, declaring that "state programs that are wholly neutral in offering educational assistance to a class defined without reference to religion do not violate" the primary effect test.[15] Justice Powell also emphasized that such programs should not be viewed in isolation, but rather that the proper inquiry must encompass "the nature and consequences of the program *viewed as a whole*."[16] That observation would prove helpful in the Cleveland case, in which the Court viewed the scholarship program in the broader context of school choices available to Cleveland families.

The next case, *Zobrest*, began to blur the lines between

14. Despite the decisive win, Witters came away empty-handed. When the case was remanded, the use of the aid was invalidated by the Washington Supreme Court under the "Blaine amendment" of its state constitution, discussed infra.

15. *Witters*, 474 U.S. at 490–91 (Powell, J., concurring).

16. Id., p. 492 (emphasis in original).

direct and indirect aid. In that case, a school district refused to provide an interpreter for a deaf student attending a Catholic high school, to which he would have been entitled if he had chosen a public or nonsectarian private school, on the grounds that it would violate the First Amendment. After all, the district asserted, the interpreter would sign religious as well as secular lessons. *Zobrest* raised a crucial question: would aid have to be segregated between religious and nonreligious instruction? If so, it surely would trigger the third part of the Establishment Clause test, excessive entanglement between the state and religion.[17] Fortunately for subsequent school choice programs, the answer was no. Again the Court assessed the issue in terms of indirectness of the aid: the fact that a child is attending a religious school and receiving religious instruction "cannot be attributed to state decisionmaking."[18]

The *Zobrest* dissenters focused on the symbolism created by a public school employee interpreting lessons in a religious school, which in their view raised the specter of state sponsorship. Because of that special problem, *Zobrest* in some ways presented a tougher case than a school choice program, which imparts no physical indicia of state sponsorship. Indeed, perhaps unwittingly, the dissenters acknowledged as much. Justice Harry Blackmun, joined by Justice David Souter, objected to the symbolic message implied when a public employee who was involved "in the teaching and propagation of religious doctrine." By contrast, the dissenters aptly observed, "[w]hen government dispenses public funds to individuals who employ them to finance private choices, it is difficult to argue that government is actually endorsing

17. The excessive governmental entanglement prong of the *Lemon* test provides an important safeguard against legitimate libertarian concerns about government regulation of private schools in school choice programs.

18. *Zobrest*, 509 U.S. at 10.

religion."[19] Unfortunately, that probative insight would elude Justice Souter nine years later in *Zelman*.

Rosenberger buttressed the neutrality principle even more. The University of Virginia excluded student-sponsored religious publications from support from student fees on the grounds that it would violate the First Amendment to include them. To the contrary, the Court ruled: it violates the First Amendment to *exclude* them, an act that constitutes impermissible content-based speech discrimination. The Court applied its now-familiar Establishment Clause framework to find that financial support for religious publications, within the broader context of student activities, did not have the primary effect of advancing religion.

The criteria set forth in *Mueller* and subsequent cases seemed hospitable to school choice programs. By definition, such programs are indirect in that funds flow to religious schools only if parents choose to send their children there. Neutrality is slightly more difficult if states already provide public school choices or if suburban schools are unwilling to participate. If the courts were willing to look at the broader context of school choices, such as open public school enrollment or charter schools, the neutrality criterion could easily be satisfied. And all of the contemporary school choice programs were designed with the Supreme Court's framework in mind.

The two most recent cases—*Agostini*, involving the provision of public school teachers for remedial instruction in religious schools, and *Mitchell*, which considered computers and other materials for aid-eligible students in religious schools— also authorized neutral aid but created some uncertainty. Because the aid was provided directly to schools for eligible

19. Id. at 22–23 (Blackmun, J., dissenting).

students, the Court considered it relevant whether public funds "ever reach the coffers of religious schools."[20] *Agostini* was written for a 5–4 majority by Justice O'Connor, and it applied the same two-part framework applied in the post-*Nyquist* cases. *Agostini* signaled a willingness on the part of the Court to overrule *Nyquist*-era precedents that seemed to require discrimination against religious schools rather than neutrality. The Court also subtly modified the definition of neutrality. In *Nyquist*'s footnote 38 and in subsequent decisions, the Court had depicted neutrality as encompassing public and private choices. But in *Agostini*, the Court found that the neutrality criterion was satisfied where "the aid is allocated on the basis of neutral, secular criteria that neither favor nor disfavor religion, and is made available to both religious and secular beneficiaries on a nondiscriminatory basis."[21] School choice programs easily could satisfy that standard, even if they did not explicitly include public schools within the range of options.

But in *Mitchell*, the plurality opinion for four justices, written by Justice Clarence Thomas, determined that neutrality should be the sole criterion in aid cases. Though joining in the plurality's conclusion that the aid was permissible, Justice O'Connor concurred separately with Justice Stephen Breyer to delineate the differences between indirect ("true private choice") and direct aid programs, emphasizing again that direct aid programs may be unconstitutional if they result in public funds reaching religious school coffers. Justice O'Connor seemed merely to be reiterating the two-pronged approach—neutrality plus true private choice—that the Court had applied since *Mueller*; but her alliance with Justice Breyer,

20. *Agostini*, 521 U.S. at 228.
21. Id. at 231.

who had not previously displayed moderation on Establishment Clause issues, was worrisome. Was Justice Breyer now a possible vote in favor of school choice? Was Justice O'Connor a possible vote against?

The Cleveland Program

It was amidst that uncertainty—a congenial constitutional standard but a closely divided Court—that the Cleveland case went up to the U.S. Supreme Court, with the future of educational freedom at stake.

The Cleveland program arose amidst a chronically mismanaged school system whose control had been seized by a federal court from local officials and transferred to the state. When the program was enacted in 1995, Cleveland students had a one-in-14 chance of graduating on time with senior-level proficiency and a one-in-14 chance of being a victim of crime inside the public schools each year. The state responded in part with an array of educational options, including the Cleveland scholarship program.[22]

The Cleveland scholarship program was designed to satisfy the Court's Establishment Clause criteria. Eligible students, defined by residence and family income, could direct a portion of their state education funds as full payment of tuition at participating schools. Both private schools inside Cleveland and public schools in the surrounding suburbs were invited to par-

22. Milwaukee has the oldest urban school choice program for low-income students, dating to 1990. It was expanded in 1995 to include religious schools. Florida created a statewide choice program for students in failing public schools in 1999. Arizona enacted scholarship tax credits, by which taxpayers can receive a tax credit for contributions to private scholarship funds, a program that subsequently has been emulated by Pennsylvania and Florida. All those programs and others were taken into consideration in the U.S. Supreme Court's deliberations over the Cleveland program.

ticipate. Private schools would receive a maximum of $2,500 per student; suburban public schools would receive approximately $6,000. Unfortunately, although all private schools in Cleveland signed up for the program, no suburban public schools did. Moreover, the two largest nonsectarian private schools in the program converted to community (charter) school status, thereby receiving about twice as much reimbursement as they had in the scholarship program. As a result, approximately 82 percent of the schools in the program were religious, enrolling about 96 percent of the scholarship students.

A panel of the U.S. Court of Appeals for the Sixth Circuit, by a 2–1 vote, found that those facts amounted to a violation of the Establishment Clause.[23] In assessing the program's neutrality, the court did not examine the program on its face, but instead looked at the percentages of religious schools in the program and the students attending them. The court viewed the scholarship program in isolation, declining to consider the broader context of school choices, including publicly funded private nonsectarian community schools. The court also concluded that no true private choice existed, because few of the participating schools were nonsectarian. That fact the court attributed to the small amount of the scholarship and the state's failure to compel suburban public schools to participate.

In taking the case to the Supreme Court, we expected one of the following outcomes: (1) the Court would issue an opinion broadly validating school choice; (2) the Court would strike down the program based on some peculiar aspect of its design, providing a road map for future school choice programs; or (3) the Court would uphold the program, but the majority would

23. *Simmons-Harris v. Zelman*, 234 F.3d 945 (6th Cir. 2000). Previously the Ohio Supreme Court had reached the opposite result; *Simmons-Harris v. Goff*, 711 N.E.2d 203 (Ohio 1999).

factionalize, as in *Mitchell*, thereby depriving us of a clear rule of law. Based on recent precedents, we did not think the Court would broadly disavow school choice. Any of the likely outcomes would give us greater certainty; but of course the first one—a clear and decisive victory—would have the greatest beneficial impact for school choice. And that, of course, is what school choice advocates aimed to achieve.

Knowing that the State of Ohio would exhaustively confront the Establishment Clause issues, we decided to take a more expansive approach in our brief.[24] First we moved to blunt the plaintiffs' tactical advantage of defining the terms of the debate. We sought to do that by setting forth crucial "background principles" that should inform the Court's deliberation. The case did not merely implicate religious establishment issues, we argued. It also raised important considerations of federalism, parental liberty, and equal educational opportunities, all of which are values deeply embedded in our nation's constitutional tradition, and which were promoted by expanding parental choice and educational options. Moreover, the First Amendment contains not only a prohibition against religious establishment but also a guarantee of the free exercise of religion. That combination translates appropriately, as the Court has recognized, into a requirement of nondiscrimination, or neutrality, toward religion. Again, we suggested, the program serves the principle of nondiscrimination, whereas the exclusion of religious schools would violate it.

We then went on to address the "primary effect" criterion in real-world terms. The Cleveland scholarship program grew out of a severe crisis in the Cleveland City Public Schools, whose administration had been turned over to the state by fed-

24. I discuss our litigation strategy in much greater detail in Clint Bolick, *Voucher Wars: Waging the Litigation Battle Over School Choice* (Washington, D.C.: Cato Institute, 2003).

eral court order, and which in the previous school year had satisfied zero out of 28 state performance criteria. The program sought to enlist the widest possible range of educational options, and it operates within a broad array of public educational choices. The program's neutrality, we urged, should be determined on its face, not on the basis of statistics, for two reasons. First, hitching a program's constitutionality to the actions of third parties renders the process hopelessly subjective; and indeed, third parties (such as suburban public schools) could effectively veto the constitutionality of a program by refusing to participate. It seemed perverse that because some schools refused to throw inner-city youngsters an educational life preserver, then no schools would be allowed to do so. Second, statistics can change from year to year.

Moreover, the program should be evaluated not in isolation, we argued, but in its broader context. We presented a study by education researcher Jay Greene showing that if all schools of choice in Cleveland, including magnet and community schools, were taken into account, only 16.5 percent of Cleveland schoolchildren were enrolled in religious schools of choice. If the state had adopted all the choice programs at one time, under a statistical standard the program unquestionably would be constitutional. Why should it matter that the state adopted different options one step at a time? We introduced evidence showing that after the litigation ceased in Milwaukee, the number of nonsectarian private schools participating in the program—and the percentage of children attending them—increased substantially. We also cited affidavits and studies demonstrating the educational effects of school choice, showing again that the program's primary effect was not to advance religion but to expand educational opportunities for children who desperately needed them.

Finally, we argued that the program marked no revolution

in Establishment Clause jurisprudence. Others who were involved in the litigation were interested in reforming that area of the law, urging the Court to overrule *Nyquist*, or even *Lemon*. We always have taken a much more conservative approach: our goal is to defend school choice programs, rather than to remake Establishment Clause law. So we urged that *Nyquist* need not be overruled. To the contrary, school choice presented an easier case than the programs presented in *Agostini* and *Mitchell*, because the transmission of aid depends entirely on the independent decisions of parents. That characteristic attenuates any perception of state endorsement of religion, a recurrent Establishment Clause concern.

In sum, our approach and that of our allies was to depict the case as one about education, not religion. The plaintiffs inadvertently gave sanction to that argument through their mere identity: teachers unions, after all, care little about religious establishment, but greatly about educational policy. And if the program really was about education, we reasoned, then its "primary effect" could not be to advance religion.

Supreme Decision

The Court's decision vindicated the most optimistic hopes of school choice supporters. Though a 5–4 decision, the Court majority spoke with a single, decisive voice, providing precisely the clarity necessary for the school choice movement to progress. Inexplicably, Justice Breyer retreated from the framework set forth in his *Mitchell* concurrence; but Justice O'Connor remained true. Writting the decision for the majority,[25] Chief Justice Rehnquist moderated his position from

---

25. It was fitting that the chief justice wrote the majority, for he also wrote the *Mueller* decision in 1983, which inaugurated the modern era of Establishment Clause jurisprudence.

Mitchell, accommodating Justice O'Connor by retaining the "true private choice" criterion that the *Mitchell* plurality sought to jettison.

In addition to Rehnquist, four justices fully joined the majority opinion: O'Connor, Anthony Kennedy, Scalia, and Thomas. The chief justice began by recounting the grievous educational conditions giving rise to the Cleveland scholarship program. It was against that backdrop, the Court observed, that the scholarship program was adopted as "part of a broader undertaking by the State to enhance the educational options of Cleveland's schoolchildren" in response to the education crisis.[26] The Court examined other educational options, including magnet and community schools, as well as the higher dollar amount they commanded. The Court did not suggest that such options were essential to the constitutionality of the choice program, but merely illustrated that when the legislature enacted the school choice program, it was simply adding religious schools to a broader range of secular educational alternatives.

Applying the law, Rehnquist observed that "our decisions have drawn a consistent distinction between government programs that provide aid directly to religious schools . . . and programs of true private choice, in which government aid reaches religious schools only as a result of the genuine and independent choices of private individuals."[27] Whereas the Court's recent cases had expanded the permissible realm of direct aid, "our jurisprudence with respect to true private choice programs has remained consistent and unbroken."[28] Recounting that jurisprudence, Chief Justice Rehnquist declared that "where a government aid program is neutral with

26. *Zelman v. Simmons-Harris*, 122 S. Ct. at 2464.
27. Id. at 2465.
28. Id. at 2466.

respect to religion, and provides assistance to a broad class of citizens who, in turn, direct government aid to religious schools wholly as a result of their own genuine and independent private choice, [it] is not readily subject to challenge under the Establishment Clause."[29]

The Court was convinced that the program was both neutral and "a program of true private choice," as part of "a general and multifaceted undertaking by the State of Ohio to provide educational opportunities to the children of a failed school district."[30] "It confers educational assistance directly to a broad class of individuals defined without reference to religion."[31] Moreover, "[t]he program permits the participation of *all* schools within the district, religious or nonreligious. Adjacent public schools also may participate and have a financial incentive to do so."[32] By contrast, the program did not provide a financial incentive for parents to choose religious schools; to the contrary, it creates "financial *dis*incentives for religious schools."[33] Parents receiving scholarships have to co-pay a part of their tuition ($250), whereas parents choosing traditional, magnet, or community schools pay nothing. Emphasizing that although "such features of the program are not necessary to its constitutionality," they "clearly dispel" any notion that the program is skewed toward religion.[34]

Citing the Greene study, the Court viewed the program in the broader context of school choices, and rejected the statistical snapshot as a touchstone of constitutionality: "The Establishment Clause question is whether Ohio is coercing parents

29. Id. at 2467.
30. Id. at 2467–68.
31. Id. at 2468 (citations omitted).
32. Id. (emphasis in original).
33. Id. (emphasis in original).
34. Id.

into sending their children to religious schools, and that question must be answered by evaluating *all* options Ohio provides Cleveland schoolchildren, only one of which is to obtain a private scholarship and then choose a religious school."[35] Beyond that, the Court emphasized, "The constitutionality of a neutral educational aid program simply does not turn on whether and why, in a particular area, at a particular time, most private schools are run by religious organizations, or most recipients choose to use the aid at a religious school."[36]

Finally, the Court confronted *Nyquist*, finding no reason to overrule it because it did not compel the Court to strike down the program. After all, *Nyquist* involved programs that were designed unmistakably to aid religious schools, and the Court expressly had left open the question—answered subsequently in *Mueller* and other cases—of the constitutionality of a genuinely neutral aid program. Hence, the Court's ruling changed jurisprudence not at all.

In closing, the Court underscored the moderation of its decision:

> In sum, the Ohio program is entirely neutral with respect to religion. It provides benefits directly to a wide spectrum of individuals, defined only by financial need and residence in a particular school district. It permits such individuals to exercise genuine choice among options public and private, secular and religious. The program is therefore a program of true private choice. In keeping with an unbroken line of decisions rejecting challenges to similar programs, we hold that the program does not offend the Establishment Clause.[37]

Justice O'Connor wrote separately to emphasize two points: that the decision does not mark "a dramatic break from

---

35. Id. at 2469 (emphasis in original).
36. Id. at 2470.
37. Id. at 2473.

the past," and that the inquiry regarding "true private choice" should "consider all reasonable educational alternatives to religious schools that are available to parents."[38] In the overall context of school choices in Cleveland, Justice O'Connor emphasized, religious schools played a small role. Moreover, government policies in general, including tax exemptions for religious institutions, already bestow a substantial financial benefit. That context, she explained, "places in broader perspective the alarmist claims about implications of the Cleveland program" sounded by the dissenters.[39]

Justice Thomas's concurring opinion was especially poignant, remarking that "[t]oday many of our inner-city public schools deny emancipation to urban minority students," who "have been forced into a system that continually fails them."[40] He observed, "While the romanticized ideal of universal public education resonates with the cognoscenti who oppose vouchers, poor urban families just want the best education for their children, who will certainly need it to function in our high-tech and advanced society."[41] The Cleveland scholarship program, he concluded, "does not force any individual to submit to religious indoctrination or education. It simply gives parents a greater choice as to where and in what manner to educate their children. This is a choice that those with greater means have routinely exercised."[42]

Displaying a penchant for original intent jurisprudence that makes him one of the Court's greatest modern justices, Justice Thomas also raised the question whether the Establishment Clause should be construed to limit state action. By its

38. Id. (O'Connor, J., concurring).
39. Id. at 2475.
40. Id. at 2480 (Thomas, J., concurring).
41. Id. at 2483.
42. Id. at 2482.

terms, the First Amendment is addressed to Congress. Most of the provisions of the Bill of Rights have been "incorporated" to apply to the states through the Fourteenth Amendment. But as Justice Thomas observed, "When rights are incorporated against the States through the Fourteenth Amendment they should advance, not constrain, individual liberty."[43] He concluded that "[t]here would be a tragic irony in converting the Fourteenth Amendment from a guarantee of opportunity to an obstacle against education reform [that] distorts our constitutional values and disserves those in the greatest need."[44]

Justices John Paul Stevens, Souter, and Breyer penned strident dissents. All of them rejected the Establishment Clause framework that the Court has applied for the past two decades. Justice Stevens raised concerns about "religious strife," raising the specter of "the Balkans, Northern Ireland, and the Middle East"[45]—concerns echoed by Justice Souter's claims of "divisiveness"[46] and Justice Breyer's warnings of "religiously based conflict"[47]—all notwithstanding that, as the majority pointed out, "the program has ignited no 'divisiveness' or 'strife' other than this litigation."[48] Nor, as the majority observes, do the dissenters propose any rule of law by which the Court could discern when a program is too religiously divisive to sustain.

The fact is that the government already dispenses billions of dollars through the G.I. Bill, Pell Grants, student loans, and other programs that can be used for religious education. Yet Americans are not at each other's throats in religious conflict.

43. Id. at 2481.
44. Id. at 2482.
45. Id. at 2485 (Stevens, J., dissenting).
46. Id. at 2502 (Souter, J., dissenting).
47. Id. at 2508 (Breyer, J., dissenting).
48. Id. at 2472 n. 7.

The reason that we do not see strife is that allowing benefits to be used in a nondiscriminatory fashion and directed by individual choice actually promotes a value that liberals are supposed to support: diversity. No one views a Pell Grant used at Georgetown or Yeshiva University as primarily advancing religion, because of the plethora of available options. Nor have the Cleveland, Milwaukee, or Florida school choice programs created religious strife, because they correctly are perceived as educational programs. By engaging in totally unfounded hyperbole, the dissenters undercut their own credibility.

The main dissenting opinion, written by Justice Souter and signed by Justices Stevens, Ruth Bader Ginsburg, and Breyer, castigated the Court's jurisprudence beginning with *Mueller*. It also concluded that no true private choice exists in Cleveland, but that instead parents are presented with a "Hobson's choice."[49] The dissenters on this point maintain that the public schools are so bad—and the religious schools by comparison so good—that Cleveland parents have no realistic choice. It seems odd that the proposed solution would be to eliminate the only positive choice. Justice Souter concedes that in his view there is nothing the state permissibly can do to make religious options available. "The majority notes that I argue both that the Ohio program is unconstitutional because the voucher amount is too low to create real private choice and that any greater expenditure would be unconstitutional as well," he observes. "The majority is dead right about this."[50] For the dissenters, the only constitutionally permissible option is for the state to consign students to government schools, no matter how defective.

49. Id., p. 2497 (Souter, J., dissenting).
50. Id., p. 2496 n. 16.

Moving to the verge of panic, the dissenters warn that "the amount of federal aid that may go to religious education after today's decision is startling: according to one estimate,[51] the cost of a national voucher program would be $73 billion, 25% more than the current national public-education budget."[52] It is comforting that the four liberal justices have suddenly assumed the role of guardians of the public fisc; but as a matter of factual analysis and Establishment Clause jurisprudence, it is off base. Not only does the government already spend a great deal on private education—not just at the post-secondary level but at the elementary and secondary levels through the Individuals with Disabilities Education Act—but private school education in the lower grades can actually save the government money (as witness the $2,250 expended for full payment of private school tuition in the Cleveland program). Moreover, Establishment Clause jurisprudence never has turned upon the amount of money spent (in the view of rigid separationists, one dollar is too much) but rather upon whether government coercion is present. The dissenters would return us to an era in which the U.S. Supreme Court grafted upon the Constitution a requirement of discrimination against religion, perhaps one in which, imagining the unfathomable, a court might even rule it impermissible for a public school to sponsor a salute to the American flag because it contains the words "under God"!

Finally, the four dissenters take up the role of lobbyists, beseeching the "political branches [to] save us from the consequences of the majority's decision," and expressing the

51. You guessed it: the "projection" is from the militantly anti–school choice People for the American Way, whose studies are copiously cited by the dissenters, although they are not part of the case record.
52. *Zelman*, p. 2498 n. 20 (Souter, J., dissenting).

"hope that a future Court will reconsider today's dramatic departure from basic Establishment Clause principle."[53]

Not content with Justice Souter's 34-page opus, Justice Breyer presented a separate dissent, joined by Justices Stevens and Souter (but curiously, not by Justice Ginsburg). He wrote separately "because I believe that the Establishment Clause concern for protecting the Nation's social fabric from religious conflict poses an overriding obstacle to the implementation of this well-intentioned school voucher program."[54] For Justice Breyer, it is not enough to vindicate the express intent of the First Amendment—to prohibit laws "respecting an establishment of religion"—but also to avoid "religiously based social conflict."[55] In this regard, it doesn't seem to matter that the program, in its sixth year of existence, has not created religious conflict, nor that its aim is educational. Instead, Breyer views the program against the backdrop of religious strife both in the United States and abroad. Helpfully, he informs us that in the United States, "Major religions include, among others, Protestants, Catholics, Jews, Muslims, Buddhists, Hindus, and Sikhs. . . . And several of these major religions contain different subsidiary sects with different religious beliefs."[56] Apparently, the only way we can all get along is if each group is denied the opportunity to direct government benefits as they see fit—or, even worse, to direct them across religious lines, as with the large percentage of non-Catholic families sending their children in inner-city Catholic schools.

Justice Breyer concedes that the "consequence" of existing aid programs that include religious options "has not been great

---

53. Id. at 2502. Justice Souter took the additional dramatic step of reading his dissent from the bench.

54. Id. (Breyer, J., dissenting).

55. Id. at 2505.

56. Id.

turmoil."[57] Nor is there evidence that the Cleveland program—or any other school choice program—has caused religious strife. But a voucher program, in Justice Breyer's view, "risks creating a form of religiously based conflict potentially harmful to the Nation's social fabric."[58] Note the hypothetical language: it does not *do* it, it only *risks* it; and what it risks is not invariable harm but *potential* harm. On this double hypothesis, the dissenters would substitute their abstract concerns for the State of Ohio's urgent effort to deliver educational opportunities in the all-too-real bedlam of Cleveland.

One wonders whether, in five years, or ten, when the dire prognostications of religious strife pass unfulfilled, the dissenters would reconsider their opinions. Likewise, it is curious that the dissenters focused on an argument that the plaintiffs made only in passing. The plaintiffs focused mainly on efforts to shoehorn the Cleveland program into the *Nyquist* construct. The dissenters implicitly acknowledged that the past twenty years of jurisprudence firmly sanction school choice programs. Instead, they embraced an ends-justifies-the-means rationale that substitutes the subjective fears of individual justices for the clear command of governmental neutrality embodied in the First Amendment's religion clauses. Fortunately, that view did not prevail, but it is genuinely alarming that it attracted four votes.

The Road Ahead

Notwithstanding the dissenters' shrill rhetoric, the majority opinion is the law of the land, and it dissipates the cloud over school choice programs. All recent voucher programs and proposals readily would satisfy the applicable criteria, particu-

57. Id. at 2506.
58. Id. at 2508.

larly if they operate in a broader context of secular educational choices. Likewise, so do scholarship and tuition tax credit programs.[59] It now seems entirely permissible for the government to adopt a program in which *all* education funding is channeled through students, to public and private schools alike. The decision could help usher in an era of child-centered public education reform whereby the state is primarily a *funder* rather than a *provider* of education, focusing less on *where* children are being educated and more on *whether* children are being educated.

The immediate beneficiaries of the decision are families in school choice programs who have lived in constant fear that their children will be pried out of the only good schools they have ever attended. The anti–school choice lobby is deprived of one of its most potent legal weapons. In Florida, where litigation challenging the state's opportunity scholarship program is ongoing, the federal constitutional cause of action has evaporated.

The federal constitutional objection has presented not only a legal obstacle but also a legislative one. School choice opponents surely will continue to resist tenaciously any effort to dismantle the public school monopoly, but no longer will they be able to credibly assert that such efforts are unconstitutional, at least as a matter of federal constitutional law.

The litigation focus will shift to state constitutions. Among other provisions, forty-seven states have religious establishment provisions that are more explicit than the First Amendment. They fall into two categories. The first is "Blaine amendments," tracing back to the late nineteenth century when anti-Catholic activists succeeded in adding restrictive

---

59. Indeed, because *Mueller* is so closely on point, tax credit programs have fared more easily in litigation so far. In our three cases defending tax credits, we have not lost a single round in any court.

language to state constitutions in an effort to preserve Protestant hegemony over public schools and taxpayer funding.[60] Typically, the Blaine amendments prohibit "aid" or "support" of sectarian schools. The second is "compelled support" provisions, which prohibit the state from compelling individuals to support religion. About three dozen states have Blaine amendments, and several have both Blaine amendments and compelled support provisions. School choice opponents have challenged existing programs under such provisions in every case so far; and with the federal Establishment Clause no longer at their disposal, they will rely even more heavily upon them in the future to thwart school choice.

Whether a Blaine amendment or compelled support provision prevents school choice depends upon how it is interpreted by state courts. The commonsense perspective is that the state constitutional provisions have the same meaning as the federal constitution; after all, the First Amendment forbids "support" of religious schools just as do the state constitutions. School choice channels aid or support not to schools but to students. *Zelman* should provide enormous conceptual assistance to state courts interpreting such constitutional provisions.

And indeed some state courts, such as in Wisconsin and Arizona, have construed their constitutional provisions in harmony with the First Amendment, finding that school choice programs do not aid or support private schools but instead aid and support students.[61] In its decision upholding scholarship

---

60. See, e.g., Joseph P. Viteritti, "Blaine's Wake: School Choice, the First Amendment, and State Constitutional Law," 21 Harv. J. L. & Pub. Pol'y 657 (1998).

61. *Jackson v. Benson*, 578 N.W.2d 602 (Wisc.), cert. denied, 525 U.S. 997 (1998); *Kotterman v. Killian*, 972 P.2d 606 (Ariz.), cert. denied, 528 U.S. 921 (1999).

tax credits, the Arizona Supreme Court expressly recognized that "the Blaine Amendment was a clear manifestation of religious bigotry," which constrained the Court to interpret it narrowly.[62] But at least a dozen states have interpreted their constitutions as forbidding aid to students in religious schools, and others are very much in question. In Florida, for instance, a state court ruled after *Zelman* that the state's opportunity scholarship program fell under its Blaine Amendment.[63]

Interpretations of state constitutions that require discrimination against religious options seem plainly to violate the First Amendment's command of neutrality. As discussed earlier, the U.S. Supreme Court in *Rosenberger* rejected the University of Virginia's attempt to single out religious publications for exclusion from student fee funding. The nondiscrimination principle has deep jurisprudential roots in both freedom of speech and free exercise of religion. For instance, in *Widmar v. Vincent*,[64] the Court held that a state university that made its facilities generally available to the public could not prevent use of the facilities for religious worship. The Court reached a similar decision allowing religious groups to use meeting spaces in public schools in *Lamb's Chapel v. Center Moriches Union Free District*.[65] Moreover, the Court signaled that it was cognizant of the history of the Blaine amendments when the plurality remarked in *Mitchell v. Helms* that "hostility to aid to pervasively sectarian schools has a shameful pedigree that we do not hesitate to disavow."[66]

Fortunately, the *Zelman* decision allows the school choice

---

62. *Kotterman* at 624.
63. *Holmes v. Bush*, No. CV 99-3370, slip op. (Fla. Cir. Ct. Aug. 5, 2002).
64. 454 U.S. 263 (1981).
65. 508 U.S. 384 (1993); accord, *Good News Club v. Milford Central School*, 533 U.S. 98 (2001).
66. *Mitchell*, 530 U.S. at 828.

movement, for the first time in twelve years, to shift from defense to offense in the courts. Rather than fighting the Blaine Amendment issue state-by-state, we will seek a U.S. Supreme Court precedent establishing that state constitutional provisions that discriminate against religious options are themselves unconstitutional under the First Amendment. That opportunity will arise in the U.S. Supreme Court term that begins in October 2003. The Court will review the decision of the U.S. Court of Appeals for the Ninth Circuit in *Davey v. Locke*,[67] which held that the State of Washington's exclusion of theology students from otherwise available college student aid violates the First Amendment. The state justified the discrimination under its Blaine Amendment, but the Ninth Circuit ruled that the state constitution must yield to the neutrality principle of the federal constitution. A favorable precedent in the U.S. Supreme Court would establish that states may not discriminate against religious school options, rendering Blaine amendments harmless. An adverse decision would mean that we must continue litigating Blaine amendments state-by-state, as we presently are doing in defending school choice programs in Florida and Colorado.

State constitutions can provide opportunities for school choice as well. The school choice movement can now argue forcefully that instead of remedies calling for more money, cases of educational deprivations under state constitutional guarantees can be remedied through vouchers. Although the federal constitution does not affirmatively create a right to education, many state constitutions guarantee public education that is "uniform," "thorough and efficient," "high quality," or consistent with some other standard. In at least a dozen states, state courts have found that certain tax schemes (such as prop-

67. *Davey v. Locke*, 299 F.3d 748 (9th Cir. 2002).

erty taxation) violate those provisions because poorer school districts receive less in the way of state funds. The problem with such remedies is that they do not accrue to the intended beneficiaries of the constitutional guarantees: children. We have sought to intervene in Arizona in an ongoing "tax equity" lawsuit arguing that giving more money to failing school districts does not remedy the constitutional violation. Only a monetary damages remedy—that is, vouchers—will allow students to acquire high-quality education without delay.

Such a remedy may seem novel and radical, but it would be unusual only in the educational context. Monetary damages are the typical form of relief in torts and contracts cases. For instance, were a consumer to purchase a car that turned out to be a lemon, a court would not order a tax increase in order to give the car company more money to build a better car. Rather, it would order a refund of the consumer's money, and the consumer would purchase a different car. Viewing state constitutional guarantees as a form of "warranty" would increase public school accountability and provide real alternatives to children whose schools are failing them. Such a result would be fully compatible with *Zelman*—and with court remedies under the federal Individuals with Disabilities Education Act, under which school districts that fail to provide a free "appropriate" education to disabled students must do so in a private school.

It is remarkable that it took twelve years of intense litigation to establish the baseline principle that parents may be entrusted with the decision of how to direct the education spending devoted to their children's education. It will take much more work to establish even more ambitious principles of educational freedom; but in a free society, the task is an essential one. To paraphrase Winston Churchill, this triumph marks only the end of the beginning.

But for now, advocates of educational freedom have much to celebrate. In common cause with economically disadvantaged families, we have prevailed in our first big test in the U.S. Supreme Court. The special interest groups dedicated to the status quo are momentarily vanquished. The empire will strike back, for sure; but this decision shows that they can be beaten, that David can indeed slay Goliath.

When the unions first challenged the Cleveland scholarship program in 1997, they characterized the parents as "inconsequential conduits" for the transmission of aid to religious schools. The unions, as usual, got it exactly backward: the parents *were* inconsequential, but they no longer are. In fact, in Cleveland and Milwaukee and other pockets in America, the parents are finally, and forever, in charge.

That's exactly what threatens the education establishment so much. Let's hope it proves contagious.

4

The Need for Secular Choice

LOUIS R. COHEN and C. BOYDEN GRAY

Zelman v. *Simmons-Harris* brought to a close the battle over whether school vouchers that can be used at religious institutions inherently violate the Establishment Clause. But the fight for school vouchers is far from over. One of us (Cohen) believes that echoes of the *Zelman* fight will imperil political support unless we can achieve substantially increased participation by secular schools. And both of us foresee a new fight against voucher opponents invoking once-obscure state constitutional or statutory provisions known as "Blaine amendments" to prohibit the use of vouchers for parochial education programs.

Zelman and the Establishment Clause

In 1995, after the Cleveland school district fell under state control for poor performance, the State of Ohio established a Pilot Project Scholarship Program (the "Program") to provide educational choices to families with children enrolled in a school district under state control. The Program consisted of two parts: a tuition aid program and a tutorial assistance program.

Any private school—religious or secular—can participate in the Program and accept Program students, provided the school is located within the boundaries of a covered district and meets state educational standards. The private school must agree not to discriminate on the basis of race, religion, or ethnic background or to "advocate or foster unlawful behavior or teach hatred of any person or group on the basis of race, ethnicity, national origin, or religion." Any public school in an adjacent school district may participate in the Program.

The Program began operating in the 1996–97 school year. In the 1999–2000 school year, 56 private schools participated, of which 46 (82 percent) were religiously affiliated. No eligible public school elected to participate in the Program. Over 3,700 students participated in the Program, and 96 percent enrolled in religiously affiliated schools.

The Legal Issue

The issue before the Court was whether the Program violates the Establishment Clause.

The Court's Opinion

In a 5–4 decision, the Court held that the Program does not violate the Establishment Clause because it is "entirely neutral with respect to religion" and is a program "of true private choice."[1]

After stating that the Establishment Clause "prevents a State from enacting laws that have the 'purpose' or 'effect' of advancing or inhibiting religion," the Court noted that its previous decisions have consistently distinguished between gov-

---

1. Chief Justice Rehnquist wrote the Court's opinion; he was joined by Justices O'Connor, Scalia, Kennedy, and Thomas.

ernment programs that provide aid directly to religious schools, on the one hand, and programs of "true private choice" on the other (that is, where government aid reaches religious schools only as a result of the choice of private individuals). Because, the Court said, there was no dispute that the Program had been enacted for the "purpose" of providing educational assistance to poor children, the Court focused its inquiry on whether the Program had the "effect" of advancing or inhibiting religion.

Drawing from three previous decisions,[2] the Court said that "where a government aid program is neutral with respect to religion, and provides assistance directly to a broad class of citizens who, in turn, direct government aid to religious schools wholly as a result of their own genuine and independent private choice, the program is not readily subject to challenge under the Establishment Clause." The Court found that the constitutional inquiry did not turn on "whether and why, in a particular area, at a particular time, most private schools are run by religious organizations, or most recipients choose to use the aid at a religious school." As a result, the fact that 96 percent of the students participating in the Program enrolled in religiously affiliated schools did not factor heavily into the inquiry.[3] The Court held that, despite the overwhelm-

---

2. *Zobrest v. Catalina Foothills School Dist.*, 509 U.S. 1 (1993) (upholding a federal program permitting sign-language interpreters to assist deaf children enrolled in religious schools); *Witters v. Washington Dept. of Servs. for the Blind*, 474 U.S. 481 (1986) (upholding a vocational scholarship program that provided tuition aid to a student studying to become a pastor); *Mueller v. Allen*, 463 U.S. 388 (1983) (upholding a Minnesota program authorizing tax deductions for private school tuition costs, among other things, even though 96 percent of the program's beneficiaries were parents of children attending religious schools).

3. The Court noted that the 96 percent figure itself did not take into account students enrolled in alternative community schools, magnet schools, and traditional public schools with tutorial assistance. Including those stu-

ing number of parents choosing religiously affiliated schools, the Program could survive the Establishment Clause challenge because any "incidental advancement of a religious mission, or the perceived endorsement of a religious message, is reasonably attributable to the individual recipient, not to the government."

Other Opinions

Justice O'Connor joined the Court's opinion, but wrote separately to emphasize her beliefs that (1) the Court's decision did not mark a "dramatic break from the past," and (2) the inquiry should consider, as a factual matter, all educational alternatives available to parents in addition to religious schools. Agreeing with the Court's statement that the inquiry must turn on the educational options actually available to parents rather than on a review of the choices the individuals ultimately make, Justice O'Connor found that after considering all the educational options available, parents have sufficient nonreligious educational options to make the Program constitutional.

Justice Thomas joined the Court's opinion but also said, in a fairly dramatic departure from recent writing about the Establishment Clause, that states may have greater latitude than the federal government because the Fourteenth Amendment is concerned primarily with "individual liberty."

Justices Stevens, Souter, Ginsberg, and Breyer dissented, arguing that the Program is, at bottom, a very large transfer of state funds to religious organizations, where the funds can be used for religious purposes.

---

dents in the denominator would drop the figure from 96 percent to under 20 percent.

The Politics of the Next Steps

One of us—Cohen—believes that school voucher programs are still very much threatened by the notion that school vouchers amount to government support of religious instruction. Supporters of school vouchers should now devote themselves to drastically enlarging secular-school participation, because the success of voucher programs almost surely depends on it.

Cohen thinks the victory in *Zelman*, while dramatic, was thin, and not just in headcount. Although the majority aimed at a ruling that could be said to rest on a "structural" interpretation of the First Amendment's Establishment Clause—that is, no impermissible *purpose* of enhancing religion plus no impermissible *effect* of enhancing religion equals no constitutional violation—the opinion depends for much of its persuasiveness on the facts of this particular case. First of all, not only were the conditions in Cleveland's inner-city schools uniquely terrible, but there also had been a state legislative determination of their terribleness. As the Court painted the picture, this case was like a drowning emergency, where the usual strategy is to throw every handy loose object in the general direction of the victim and hope something keeps him afloat. A lot of people, with a wide range of views about the First Amendment, are prepared to look at a situation like Cleveland's and say, "OK, let's try whatever anybody can think of." In Cohen's view, it is not clear that a future Supreme Court, perhaps one with a somewhat changed composition, will view *Zelman* as controlling in the context of broader programs not targeted at clear and conceded emergencies.

Moreover, at least by the time *Zelman* got to the Supreme Court, it was also conceded (and the Court explicitly assumed) that the Ohio program *was* a good-faith effort, undertaken to start resolving a difficult secular problem, and not undertaken to promote religious instruction. But a program's purposes are a question of fact. Future cases where there is a dispute about a program's basic motives will present issues the Supreme Court did not need to resolve in *Zelman* and the opinion in *Zelman* will not necessarily determine their outcomes.

Finally, the majority conclusion rested on the key determination that enrollment in religious schools was the product of "true private choice." The majority was able to determine this, to its own satisfaction, because it found that the state had made available a range of other, secular, alternatives to the failing schools. But the existence of "true private choice" is also a question of fact, on which courts could reach different conclusions under different programs, or even under the Ohio program as the evidence changes with greater experience. Even more important, the Supreme Court supported its finding in *Zelman* of "true private choice" by stressing, in both Chief Justice Rehnquist's majority opinion and Justice O'Connor's concurrence, that the Ohio program was being judged in its early days, that the litigation itself had impeded its development, and that there was evidence suggesting that additional secular schools may start up, or open up places to transferee students, in response to this and other voucher programs. If this fails to happen, opponents will mount vigorous future attacks on *Zelman*.

The four-Justice minority went further than Court minorities usually do to invite such attacks. All three dissents, by Justices Stevens, Souter, and Breyer, end with rather ringing assertions that the Court has lost its way on a point fundamental to American society, and Justice Souter's opinion, joined by all three of the other dissenters, strongly suggests that they would vote to overturn *Zelman* tomorrow if they had a fifth vote.

Cohen's fear that school vouchers are still vulnerable to

anti–Establishment Clause objections is not, however, based primarily on the risk that *Zelman* itself will someday be overturned. The emotion-stirring issues covered by the Establishment Clause are political as well as legal. School voucher programs may not have sufficient political momentum to grow if their perceived effect is to promote primarily religious instruction. Many state legislatures just won't get involved, and others will limit themselves to applying rather small Band-Aids to obvious and gaping wounds. The result will be isolated accomplishments that participants in particular communities can be proud of, but no real program for attacking the widespread deficiencies of public schools.

Organizations that are on the front lines of big constitutional battles often have very categorical views, and it is easy to see the clash of these views as the heart of the issue. In the school voucher fight, for example, some proponents would stress—and would not compromise—the view that equal treatment of religious and secular institutions is right, and the companion view that the principle of "true private choice" is close to the heart of what the Religion Clauses of the First Amendment are about. Some opponents would of course invoke the supposed "wall of separation" between church and state, and be equally unwilling to compromise. The result in *Zelman*, thought of simply as a constitutional case, was a big (if narrow) victory for one theory over the other.

But voucher *programs* are not just a matter of constitutional theory. Their success depends on state legislative action, including state funding. That means they depend on popular support, which in turn depends on how the *public* views the very issues we are talking about—the need for experimentation and competition to solve school problems, the proper role of government programs in creating or assisting alternatives to traditional public schools, and the proper role of religious institutions among those alternatives. The Supreme Court can to some extent guide public views on these issues: the Court may follow the election returns, as Mr. Dooley said, but voters follow the Court, too.

But voters have their own views on these issues, which will be shaped by the developing facts. Viewing the facts from the Supreme Court's perspective in *Zelman*, in the early days of a sincere response to an acknowledged crisis, many voters surely do favor what the Court did. It is easy for a voter to favor a program labeled as experimental, adopted in response to what everyone perceives as a true emergency, especially when the program does not cost very much. The voter may also rather easily say to herself, "That inner-city kid is probably better off—and less likely to grow up to be a menace to *me*—in a religious school with strong discipline, even if the religion is neither my own nor his."

If we were talking about a much broader, more mature, and costly program, voters' views might be far different. A pollster would surely get far less favorable average answers if he asked taxpayers, "Are you willing to have a significant portion of your state and local tax dollars spent to teach someone else's religion as part of a school curriculum for a large number of kids in your community?" Or suppose the pollster asked inner-city parents, "Are you satisfied with a state program in which the only real alternative for your child to escape the public schools is a school that teaches somebody else's religion?" Or suppose he asked people professing to be very religious, but whose denominations do not choose, or are simply too small, to support a local denominational school, "What do you think of governmental funds flowing, indirectly, to all these other denominational schools?" Or suppose he asked leaders of a church that does support a local denominational school,

"What do you think of having to admit students without regard to their religious background, and of having to teach tolerance of all religions, in some way that satisfies a state administrator, on pain of being declared ineligible for voucher funds?"

Cohen's sense is that the only way to avoid getting entangled in these issues, and facing an eventual public tide of opposition that will limit voucher programs to providing small remedies in isolated cases, is to create genuine and substantial secular educational alternatives, so that sectarian schools become a fairly small part of a larger range of choices. In other words, it is not going to be enough to have "true private choice" in the limited and technical sense that satisfied a majority of the Supreme Court. If vouchers are going to be in widespread use, they are going to have to involve a range of options that satisfies large numbers of people, including taxpayers, that they individually are getting a fair and acceptable deal.

That means designing voucher programs that will induce existing secular schools, both public and private, to accept voucher students. In *Zelman*, the Supreme Court discussed and rejected the argument that the subsidy level was insufficient to attract into the program any schools that are not parishioner supported—that is, in essence, willing to educate inner-city youth precisely because of their religious missions. But the Supreme Court, as is often the case, did not have to deal with the real world. Its 5–4 determination that the subsidy numbers did not make out a constitutional claim was not the same as a determination that there is practical reason to expect that increasing numbers of secular places will become available. In Cohen's view, proponents of vouchers need to work on that practical problem, because a program that ends up sending kids largely to religious institutions isn't going to be allowed, by the public, to grow beyond its cradle.

Blaine Amendments

In a majority of states, protracted legal battles will ensue over the Blaine amendments and their restrictions on aid to religious schools. These amendments come to us with a dark historical pedigree.[4]

Blaine Amendments: A Short Primer

During the first half of the nineteenth century, with the growth of public or common schools, educators such as Horace Mann sought to ensure that the schools were nonsectarian. But by this they did not mean secular. They believed "that moral education should be based on the common elements of Christianity to which all Christian sects would agree or to which they would take no exception," including the "reading of the Bible as containing the common elements of Christian morals but reading it with no comment in order not to introduce sectarian biases."[5] As Catholic immigrants grew in numbers throughout the nation, however, they began to complain that what was called "nonsectarian" was in fact a form of "common" Protestantism focused on individual interpretation of the Bible.

As the numbers of Irish, German, and other European Catholic and Jewish immigrants surged, so did nativist sentiments across the country, spurring the growth of organized nativist

---

4. This section of our paper is based substantially on Eric W. Treene's article titled "The Grand Finale Is Just the Beginning: School Choice and the Coming Battle Over Blaine Amendments" and is used here with his permission and the permission of The Becket Fund for Religious Liberty. Mr. Treene's article was published as a Federalist Society White Paper at a meeting of the Federalist Society's Religious Liberties Practice Group at the Ave Maria Law School on March 22, 2002.

5. R. Freeman Butts, *The American Tradition in Religion and Education* (Boston: Beacon Press, 1950), p. 118.

groups. In New York, nativist societies combined to form the American Republican Party in 1843, which evolved into the powerful (and national) Know-Nothing Party in the 1850s.[6] The Know-Nothings, who pledged to oppose Catholicism and support the reading of the King James Bible in the public schools, were active throughout the country and particularly strong in the northern and border states, sending seventy-five Congressmen to Washington in 1854.[7]

Nowhere, though, was the party more successful than in Massachusetts. The elections of 1854 swept the Know-Nothing Party into power. Know-Nothings won the governorship, the entire congressional delegation, all forty seats in the Senate, and all but three of the 379 members of the House of Representatives.[8] Armed with this overwhelming mandate, they turned quickly to what Governor Henry J. Gardner called the mission to "Americanize America."[9] The Know-Nothings required the reading of the King James Bible in all common schools; they proposed constitutional amendments (which passed both houses of the legislature) that "would have deprived Roman Catholics of their right to hold public office and restricted office and the suffrage to male citizens who had resided in the country for no less than twenty-one years"; they dismissed Irish state-government workers; and they banned foreign-language instruction in the public schools.[10] Of greatest relevance to the school choice issue was that the Know-Nothings also succeeded in adding an amendment to the Massachusetts constitution, providing: "Moneys raised by taxation

6. See Lloyd P. Jorgenson, *The State and the Non-Public School, 1825–1925* (Columbia: University of Missouri Press, 1987), pp. 94–95.

7. Id., p. 71.

8. John R. Mulkern, *The Know-Nothing Party in Massachusetts* (Boston: Northeastern University Press, 1990), p. 76.

9. Id., p. 94.

10. Id., p. 102.

in the towns and cities for the support of public schools, and all moneys which may be appropriated by the state for the support of common schools . . . shall never be appropriated to any religious sect for the maintenance exclusively of its own schools."[11]

A number of other states added nonsectarian amendments to their constitutions during this period, including Wisconsin (1849), Ohio (1851), and Minnesota (1857). A number of other states passed similar measures in the form of legislation, but it would not be until the mid-1870s that the move to amend state constitutions would take hold in earnest.

After becoming more muted during the Civil War and Reconstruction, nativism raged again in the 1870s. In 1875, President Ulysses S. Grant decried the Roman Catholic Church as a source of "superstition, ambition, and ignorance." James G. Blaine, elected Speaker of the House of Representatives in 1868, sought to capitalize on the resurgence of nativism by seeking passage of the following amendment, which bears his name, to the United States Constitution:

> No State shall make any law respecting an establishment of religion, or prohibiting the free exercise thereof; and no money raised by taxation in any State for the support of public schools, or derived from any public fund therefor, nor any public lands devoted thereto, shall ever be under the control of any religious sect; nor shall any money so raised or lands so devoted be divided between religious sects or denominations.[12]

Blaine's amendment barely failed in the Congress, passing the House 180–7 but falling four votes short in the Senate. But

---

11. Massachusetts Constitution, Amendment Article XVIII (superseded by Massachusetts Constitution, Amendment Article XLVI).

12. Jorgenson, *The State and the Non-Public School*, pp. 138–39.

Blaine had his revenge, state by state. Over the next fifteen years, states either voluntarily adopted similar "Blaine amendments" to their constitutions,[13] or were forced by Congress to enact such articles as a condition of their admittance into the Union.[14] Thirty-seven state constitutions now have provisions placing some form of restriction on government aid to religious schools beyond that in the U.S. Constitution.

This was the environment in which the Blaine amendments were passed. Rather than being separationist measures in the spirit of Madison and Jefferson, they reflect the fears and prejudices of later generations and were indeed the very opposite of separation. They were unabashed attempts to use the public school to inculcate the religious views and values of the majority and to suppress minority, or "sectarian," faiths.

The Next Battleground over School Choice

The Blaine amendments are all variations on the basic text of James Blaine's original proposed amendment and tend to be more specific than the "under the control of" language in his original. Some of the Blaine amendments have little or no case law interpreting them. Others have been interpreted to be limited in scope. But many have been expansively construed to bar forms of school aid that the Supreme Court has expressly

13. See, e.g., New York Constitution, Article XI § 3 (adopted 1894); Delaware Constitution, Article X § 3 (adopted 1897); Kentucky Constitution, § 189 (adopted 1891); Missouri Constitution, Article IX § 8 (adopted 1875).

14. See, e.g., Act of Feb. 22, 1889, 25 Stat. 676, ch. 180 (1889) (enabling legislation for South Dakota, North Dakota, Montana, and Washington); Act of June 20, 1910, 36 Stat. 557 § 26 (1910) (enabling legislation for New Mexico and Arizona); Act of July 3, 1890, 26 Stat. L. 215 § 8, ch. 656 (1890) (enabling legislation for Idaho); South Dakota Constitution, Article VIII § 16; North Dakota Constitution, Article 8 § 5; Montana Constitution, Article X § 6; Washington Constitution, Article IX § 4, Article I § 11; Arizona Constittion, Article IX § 10; Idaho Constitution, Article X § 5.

upheld under the Establishment Clause. The clearest example is Washington State, which, after the Supreme Court unanimously held in *Witters v. Washington Department of Services for the Blind*[15] that it would not violate the Establishment Clause for a blind man to use state vocational training aid to attend a seminary, ruled on remand that such aid would violate the state constitution's Blaine Amendment.[16] Similarly, bus transportation to private religious schools, upheld against Establishment Clause challenge in *Everson v. Board of Education*,[17] has been invalidated by state courts interpreting their Blaine amendments,[18] as have textbook loan programs similar to the one upheld in *Board of Education v. Allen*,[19] and a proposed tax deduction for private school tuition similar to the one upheld in *Mueller v. Allen*.[20]

As these cases portend, Blaine amendments potentially could derail school choice efforts in states throughout the country. One survey of how Blaine amendments have been interpreted found that seventeen states have "restrictive" Blaine amendments, ten others have Blaine amendments of "uncertain" interpretation, and eight states have Blaine amendments "permissive" toward state aid.[21] If these numbers

15. 474 U.S. 481 (1986).

16. *Witters v. State Com'n for the Blind*, 771 P.2d 1119 (1989).

17. 330 U.S. 1 (1947).

18. See, e.g., *Epeldi v. Engelking*, 488 P.2d 860 (Idaho 1971), *cert. denied*, 406 U.S. 957 (1972).

19. 392 U.S. 236 (1968). See, e.g., *California Teachers Association v. Riles*, 632 P.2d 953 (Calif. 1981); *McDonald v. School Bd. of Yankton Indep. Sch. Dist.*, 246 N.W. 2d 113, 117 (S.D. 1985).

20. 463 U.S. 388 (1983). See *Opinion of the Justices*, 514 N.E. 2d 353 (Mass. 1987) (proposed bill to provide a tax deduction to parents for private and public school expenses would violate Massachusetts' Anti-Aid Amendment).

21. See Frank R. Kemerer, *The Constitutional Dimension of School Vouchers*, 3 Tex. Forum on Civ. Lib & Civ. Rts. 137, 181 (1998).

are correct, school choice will either be a non-starter in more than half the states or will at least face contentious litigation over the scope of such states' Blaine amendments.

The most obvious strategy is a case-by-case effort to convince courts that their state's Blaine Amendment should not be construed to bar aid to families that reaches religious schools only through parental choice. In the states with strictly interpreted Blaine amendments, however, this may not be possible. The only choice in those states is to make the Blaine Amendments disappear as a factor entirely. This could be accomplished two ways: through state constitutional amendment, or through court rulings holding that the invocation of Blaine amendments to bar school choice violates the Free Exercise Clause of the Amendment of the U.S. Constitution.

An understanding of the nefarious history of Blaine's failed amendment and the state versions that followed is critically important to the school choice movement for three reasons. First, their true purpose should be brought to light and made clear to judges who are interpreting how a given Blaine Amendment's terms should be applied. Second, in any repeal efforts, it should be made clear to the public what these provisions are: remnants of nineteenth-century bigotry hamstringing educational reform in the twenty-first century. And finally, as a handful of cases suggest, the purpose behind the original passage of the Blaine amendments makes them particularly vulnerable to challenge under the Free Exercise Clause.

Challenging the Blaine Amendments

In the school choice cases decided thus far, Blaine amendments have not proved to be much of a barrier, which is perhaps why they have been given such little attention by the media. The Ohio Supreme Court ruled, in *Simmons-Harris v.*

Goff, that its Blaine Amendment (Section 2, Article VI of the Ohio Constitution), which states that "no religious or other sect, or sects, shall ever have any exclusive right to, or control of, any part of the school funds of this state," was not violated by the Cleveland school choice plan because school funds would only reach such "sects" through the "independent decisions of parents and students."[22]

Similarly, in *Jackson v. Benson*, the Wisconsin Supreme Court found that its Blaine Amendment, which states "nor shall any money be drawn from the treasury for the benefit of religious societies, or religious or theological seminaries," was not violated by the Milwaukee school choice plan, because "for the benefit of" was to be construed strictly and did not apply to merely incidental benefits. Arizona's Supreme Court did not merely give its Blaine Amendment a narrow construction but suggested that the circumstantial evidence of its connection to the original Blaine Amendment undermined its validity. The court observed that "[t]he Blaine Amendment was a clear manifestation of religious bigotry, part of a crusade manufactured by the contemporary Protestant establishment to counter what was perceived as a growing 'Catholic menace.'"[23]

In *Chittenden Town School District v. Vermont Department of Education*[24] the Vermont Supreme Court held that school choice would violate the state constitution, but Vermont has no Blaine Amendment. It rested its decision on the state's corollary to the Establishment Clause, which holds that no person "can be compelled to . . . support any place of worship . . . contrary to the dictates of conscience." While Ohio and Wisconsin's narrowing of their Blaine amendments was encouraging to school choice supporters, *Chittenden* suggests that

22. 711 N.E.2d 203, 212 (Ohio 1999).
23. *Kotterman v. Killian*, 972 P.2d 606, 624 (Ariz. 1999).
24. 738 A.2d 539, 547 (Vt. 1999), *cert. denied*, 528 U.S. 1066 (1999).

even narrow language not directed at schools at all can be construed to encompass school choice.

As the battles begin to be waged in other Blaine states, we believe—Gray more strongly than Cohen—that the amendments will be vulnerable to challenge under the Free Exercise Clause, both because of their discrimination against religious families and because of their sordid past.

The Supreme Court consistently has held that laws that discriminate on the basis of religion violate the Free Exercise Clause, for example in *Church of the Lukumi Babalu Aye, Inc. v. City of Hialeah*.[25] The Blaine amendments arguably do just that: they bar aid to religious or "sectarian" schools while permitting identical aid to secular schools. In *Peter v. Wedl*,[26] the Eighth Circuit held that the Free Exercise Clause barred a town from denying aid to disabled children attending religious schools that they would receive if they attended private secular schools. The court in *Peter* noted that the type of aid at issue had been found to be constitutional by the Supreme Court under the Establishment Clause, and therefore separation of church and state concerns did not justify the discrimination. This holding is the converse of the First Circuit's decision in *Strout v. Albanese*, which held that Maine could exclude religious private schools from its rural tuition plan without violating the Free Exercise Clause, on the grounds that this discrimination was required by the Establishment Clause. But the First Circuit stated that, had the voucher-like aid sought by the plaintiffs *not* violated the Establishment Clause, the state of Maine's discrimination against the plaintiffs would not be permitted. Thus, after *Zelman*, such discrimination should be found to be a Free Exercise Clause violation. The Ninth Circuit

25. 508 U.S. 520 (1993).
26. 155 F.3d 992 (8th Cir. 1998).

has disagreed, however, finding on facts nearly identical to those in *Peter v. Wedl* that there was no Free Exercise violation in the denial of aid.[27]

The Ninth Circuit did, however, find that the Free Exercise Clause was violated in *Davey v. Locke*.[28] In *Davey*, a student received a scholarship from the State of Washington based on his academic performance in high school, financial income, and his attendance at college within the state.[29] The scholarship was revoked when he declared a major in theology. The Ninth Circuit concluded that the Washington program facially discriminated on the basis of religion and was therefore subject to strict scrutiny.[30] The State argued that even if the program were subject to strict scrutiny, it had a compelling state interest in adhering to its own laws and state constitution, which included a Blaine Amendment.[31] The Ninth Circuit held that "the establishment clause in Washington's Constitution [does not] excuse [Washington's] disabling Davey from receipt of the Promise Scholarship to which he was otherwise entitled under the program's objective criteria solely on account of his personal decision to pursue a degree in theology."[32] The Supreme Court has granted *certiorari* in *Davey*, and its decision (some time in the term beginning October 2003) will be an important next chapter in the voucher debate.

Now that *Zelman* has freed the school voucher debate from the uncertainty of Federal Establishment Clause violation, the battle in the states remains. Given the nefarious origins of the

27. *KDM ex rel. WJM v. Reedsport Sch. Dist.*, 196 F.3d 1046 (9th Cir. 1999), *cert. denied*, 531 U.S. 1010 (2000).
28. 299 F.3d 748 (9th Cir. 2002).
29. Id. at 750.
30. Id.
31. Id. at 758.
32. Id. at 760.

Blaine amendments, recent cases narrowing their construction, and some promising Free Exercise cases, the outlook is optimistic that eventually there will be an unfettered public policy debate about school vouchers.

5

**Liberalism
and School
Choice**

PETER BERKOWITZ

I

The debate over school choice presents a puzzling spectacle. On one side are the proponents of choice. In response to the longstanding crisis of our inner-city public schools, they favor more charter schools (schools that directly receive state funds as a result of commitments made in the school's charter). And far more controversially, they favor provision by the state of cash vouchers for parents to use (or if they prefer, not use) at participating public and private schools. In the field of education, the proponents of choice stand for innovation, experimentation, and a diversity of approaches. Interestingly, they are generally thought of as the conservatives.

On the other side are the opponents of school choice. Their response to our failing public schools is to seek to strengthen them, usually by spending more money. The opponents of

This essay draws upon "Liberals vs. Religion," *The Weekly Standard*, July 15, 2002, pp. 13–16, and "Liberal Education," ibid., May 20, 2002, pp. 35–39.

choice stand with entrenched interests, especially big city school boards and teachers unions. They defend the status quo, particularly concerning school governance. And they warn ominously that even small changes to a system that has its roots in the nineteenth century will undermine our shared civic culture. Quite interestingly, they are generally thought of as liberals or progressives.

In one respect, the apparently conservative and apparently progressive positions in the debate over school choice do line up as one would expect. The proponents of choice, in the spirit of much conservative public policy, press for market-based reforms. The opponents of choice, following in the footsteps of most progressive public policy, put their faith in the state. But there is no good reason to suppose in advance of investigation that the market always advances entrenched interests and the state is always a force for progress. Indeed, in the case of school choice there is good reason to reject these propositions.

The considerable confusion and paradox in the opposing positions in the debate over school choice testifies to the inadequacy of our political labels. It also reflects a disagreement about the facts concerning the most effective means to bettering public education, and thus the need to think through more clearly the critical question of government's role in the education of our nation's children as well as the educational role of other crucial institutions and associations, in particular the family. And it invites a reconsideration of the question that underlies much of the disagreement between the proponents and opponents of school choice: what are the ends of education in a free society?

All the confusion and paradox are on display in the United State Supreme Court's 5–4 decision in June 2002 in *Zelman v.*

Simmons-Harris[1] upholding the constitutionality of the Ohio school voucher program. Sorting things out requires not only clarifying the legal issues at stake in the case but laying bare the disagreement about the purposes of a liberal democracy that underlies both the debate about what the Constitution requires, permits, or prohibits in the area of school choice and about the educational policies that would best serve the public interest.

II

The United State Supreme Court's 5–4 decision in *Zelman* was not really as close as it seems, at least not if the quality of the constitutional arguments of the five-justice majority is weighed against the quality of the arguments of the four-justice minority. As in sports, the final score can be deceiving. But the tendencies of the bad arguments employed by the dissenters are revealing.

Commonly, progressives or left-liberals criticize conservative judges for elevating abstract principle and formal rules over the real-life situations of the disadvantaged. Yet in dissent Justices Stevens, Souter, Breyer, and Ginsburg displayed an aversion to disadvantaged people's actual choices in favor of choices made by the federal government, a strong preference for rigid principle over concrete political reality, and a strange solicitude for speculative future harm to the body politic at the expense of manifest actual harm to flesh and blood low-income citizens in the here and now. Since such tendencies seldom play so prominent a role in the thinking of the more liberal justices—they are likely to emphasize context, pragmatic considerations, and substantive justice, particularly for the least

1. 122 S. Ct. at 2460 (2002).

well off in society—what brought these tendencies to the fore in the case of school choice?

Judging by the overheated rhetoric and intellectual inadequacies of the dissents, the answer, I think, is a profound distrust of religion and the conviction that the state has an obligation to rescue citizens from its clutches.

The majority opinion, written by Chief Justice Rehnquist and joined by Justices O'Connor, Scalia, Kennedy, and Thomas, is relatively straightforward. As a response to Cleveland's failed public schools, among the very worst in the nation, Ohio crafted a school choice program. The program gives low-income urban parents a variety of options for the education of their children, including cash vouchers that parents can use if they wish to send their children to participating public schools, or participating private schools, religious or secular.

Of the parents who chose the voucher option in the 1999–2000 school year, 96 percent chose to send their children to religious private schools. But the families who chose the voucher option—about 3,700—represent only about 5 percent of the more than 75,000 eligible Cleveland families; the rest chose other options offered by the program, including community schools, magnet schools, and keeping their children in public schools and receiving tutorial aid from the state.

The majority opinion held that the Ohio program and those like it are constitutional, and do not violate the Establishment Clause of the First Amendment, so long as they are neutral in respect to religion and permit parents to exercise "true private choice." Private choice is truly exercised when "government aid reaches religious schools only as a result of the genuine and independent choices of private individuals."[2] Because of

2. *Zelman v. Simmons-Harris*, 122 S. Ct. at 2465.

the variety of options that Ohio offers Cleveland schoolchildren and their parents, no reasonable observer, held Rehnquist, could view the program as advancing or endorsing religion. In choosing to use vouchers to send their children to religious schools, Cleveland parents, stressed Justice Thomas in his concurrence, were exercising their fundamental liberty to educate their children as they deem best.

The dissenters disagreed vehemently. But among themselves they agreed that the harsh realities and unquestioned harms suffered by low-income, mostly minority schoolchildren in Cleveland should not be allowed to override the hallowed principle of strict separation of church and state for which, they asserted, the Establishment Clause has always stood.

In his dissent, Justice Stevens showed his unyielding allegiance to the principle of strict separation by going so far as to argue that the magnitude of the educational deprivation suffered by the Cleveland students and the complexity and indirectness of the interaction between church and state in the challenged program (of which the majority made much) had no bearing on the Ohio program's constitutionality. Never mind "the severe educational crisis that confronted the Cleveland City School District when Ohio enacted its voucher program,"[3] Stevens wrote. Never mind "the wide range of choices that have been made available to students *within the public school system.*"[4] And never mind "the voluntary character of the private choice to prefer a parochial education over an education in the public school system."[5] What was absolutely decisive in Justice Stevens's mind, and what rendered the "Court's decision profoundly misguided," was that in viola-

3. Id. at 2484.
4. Id.
5. Id. at 2485.

tion of the Establishment Clause, it "authorizes the use of public funds to pay for the indoctrination of thousands of grammar school children in particular religious faiths."[6]

Such indoctrination, Stevens explains, can only lead to political disaster of monumental proportions. "I have been influenced," Stevens concludes, "by my understanding of the impact of religious strife on the decisions of our forbears to migrate to this continent, and on the decision of neighbors in the Balkans, Northern Ireland, and the Middle East to mistrust one another. Whenever we remove a brick from the wall that was designed to separate religion and government, we increase the risk of religious strife and weaken the foundation of our democracy."[7]

Justice Souter, in a dissent joined by Justices Stevens, Ginsburg, and Breyer, decried the "doctrinal bankruptcy"[8] of the majority's opinion. Though he too acknowledged that the situation in the Cleveland public schools was dire, he insisted that the rigid principle of strict separation left him no choice: "If there were an excuse for giving short shrift to the Establishment Clause, it would probably apply here. But there is no excuse. Constitutional limitations are placed on government to preserve constitutional values in hard cases, like these."[9] Souter, however, did not actually find the case a hard one. In the Ohio program, he held, "every objective underlying the prohibition of religious establishment is betrayed."[10]

Indeed, for Souter the "enormity of the violation"[11] was all but unprecedented. Citing a sentence fragment from Jefferson's

6. Id.
7. Id.
8. Id. at 2486.
9. Id.
10. Id. at 2498.
11. Id.

"Bill for Establishing Religious Freedom" in Virginia, Souter appeared to embrace the uncompromising view that any tax money that in any way reaches a religious organization is antithetical to freedom.[12] Then, citing a sentence fragment from Madison's "Memorial and Remonstrance," Souter seemed to argue that every form of indirect aid to religion involves the state in the shackling of young minds.[13] And citing no authority and offering not a scintilla of evidence from any source, he warned of a political crisis stemming from the "divisiveness permitted by today's majority."[14]

Justice Breyer, in a dissent joined by Stevens and Souter, proclaimed that he wrote separately "to emphasize the risk that publicly financed voucher programs pose in terms of religiously based social conflict."[15] According to Breyer, "avoiding religiously based social conflict" has always been the underlying purpose of the Establishment Clause.[16] Citing University of Chicago law professor Philip Hamburger's exhaustively detailed new book *Separation of Church and State*, Breyer creates the impression that in the twentieth century the Court elaborated an Establishment Clause jurisprudence that strictly separated church from state in large measure to protect Catholic minorities from persecution by Protestant majorities.[17] Permitting the Ohio program, according to Breyer, represents an abandonment of the doctrine of strict separation and with it an abdication of the Court's responsibility to protect minorities. Indeed, he believes the program to be "contentious" and "divisive" and to threaten "religious strife."[18] Like Justice Sou-

12. Id. at 2499.
13. Id.
14. Id. at 2502.
15. Id.
16. Id. at 2505.
17. Id. at 2504.
18. Id. at 2507.

ter, however, he fails to offer any evidence that the Ohio program has generated these unhappy consequences or planted their seeds.

The more liberal justices, then, were in agreement that school vouchers fall afoul of the doctrine of strict separation of church and state, and that strict separation serves the core purpose of the Establishment Clause, which is to avert the breakdown of social and political life that comes from conflict over religion. This interpretation of the Establishment Clause and the doctrine of strict separation is wrong—and just why it is wrong is demonstrated at great length by the very scholarship on which Justice Breyer relied—Philip Hamburger's richly documented study of the history of the doctrine of separation of church and state.

Contrary to Justice Breyer, what Hamburger actually shows is that "the constitutional authority for separation is without historical foundation."[19] In the eighteenth century, according to Hamburger, the Establishment Clause was thought by most Americans to protect religious liberty by preventing an establishment of religion by the federal government. It was not thought to interfere with a variety of common contacts and cooperation between church and state. Indeed, the Constitution's prohibition on an establishment of religion by Congress was seen as consistent with—and a protection of—the establishments of religion that existed at the time in several states. In that context, Jefferson represented a distinctly minority view. He advanced the doctrine of strict separation as an expression of his general anticlericalism, seeking to go beyond the prohibition on national establishments to a ban on contacts and cooperation between church and state. The doctrine of

19. *Separation of Church and State* (Cambridge, Mass.: Harvard University Press, 2002), p. 481.

strict separation picked up steam in the mid-nineteenth century, and reached full speed in the twentieth century Establishment Clause cases.

Contrary again to Justice Breyer's view, however, throughout its history, Hamburger emphasizes, the doctrine of strict separation has been primarily used not to enlarge the sphere of religious liberty, which was the original purpose of the Establishment Clause, but to restrict and subvert the liberty of religious minorities. In the nineteenth and twentieth centuries strict separation of church and state was not, as Justice Breyer suggests, the principle that restrained majorities in their intolerance of Catholic minorities. Quite the contrary. As Hamburger demonstrates, strict separation was used to advance that intolerance: Protestants with nativist sympathies invoked it to deny aid to Catholic schools, while at the same time they saw it as permitting public aid to public and private schools that taught a generalized Protestantism. From the perspective of those who led the way in establishing the authority of the doctrine of strict separation in twentieth-century constitutional law, what was "divisive" was not the subtle establishment of a majority (Protestant) religion (or later the establishment of a secular orthodoxy), but the reluctance of Catholics to send their children to the majority's public schools, and thereby participate in the establishment of Protestantism (and later of secular orthodoxy). Eventually the anti-Catholic implications of the doctrine of strict separation were broadened to include a more general suspicion of all religious organizations.

So while Justice Breyer and his fellow dissenters are wrong about the historical lineage of the doctrine of strict separation and the actual purposes to which it has been put, they share a purpose with strict separationists of the past. Betraying a hostility to any religious education different from the education the majority receives, the more liberal justices use the doctrine of strict separation to limit the reach of such religious education. The hostility can be seen in their rhetorical strategy, which cuts against Court precedent: they focus on where government money ends up—religious schools—and downplay how it gets there—private decisions made by parents to improve their children's educational opportunities.

The hostility of the more liberal justices to the use of government funds at religious schools in turn often seems to be rooted in hostility to religion itself. This hostility or prejudice can be seen in Justice Stevens's equation of education at religious schools with "indoctrination." It can be seen in Justice Souter's view that religious education deprives the faithful of freedom of mind. And it can be seen in the view expressed most forcefully by Justice Breyer that religious education is incurably divisive. The not-so-subtle message of all the dissents is that religion teaches intolerance and encourages antidemocratic propensities, and for this reason the state must limit to the extent possible the flow of government money to religious schools. This view of religion, at once patronizing and frightened, does not deserve establishment as a constitutional principle.

Vouchers are not a solution to all the ills of our nation's public schools, though they can be crafted to be consistent with efforts to reform failing public schools, and indeed thoughtful proponents of vouchers see them as part of such reform. Furthermore, vouchers have held little appeal for the suburban middle class, whose members are generally satisfied with the public schools that their children attend. But vouchers and school choice receive strong support from some low-income parents who want alternatives to the broken-down public schools their state and city governments offer them. An interpretation of the Establishment Clause that forbids such programs is in tension with the imperatives of justice. As it happens, such an interpretation is also in tension with the original and more constitutionally sound understanding of the Establishment Clause. Moreover, an interpretation of religion that sees it as incurably divisive and contrary to the best interests of freedom and equality is at odds with the original and more theoretically sound understanding of the liberal tradition.

III

Just as the more liberal justices on the Supreme Court argue that school choice is unconstitutional on the basis of a flawed understanding of constitutional doctrine and American history, so, too, many liberal political opponents of school choice oppose it on the basis of factually dubious or incorrect charges about the effects of school choice on students and on public schools more generally. In fact, the evidence is mounting that the expansion of choice through charters and vouchers certainly does not diminish, and likely improves, academic achievement. Recent empirical findings, many of which have been the result of studies conducted by Paul Peterson and colleagues, strike hard at the anti-choice movement's central criticisms and more than meet its legitimate concerns.[20]

The critics see school choice as a sinister and many-sided threat to democracy. They charge that school choice programs appeal to white elites who wish to separate their children from blacks and to religious parents who wish to separate their children from the secular world; that such programs, furthermore, deprive students who take advantage of them of diversity in the classroom, weaken public schools by draining away state money and creaming off the best students, and generally sub-

20. See *Charters, Vouchers, and Public Education*, ed. Paul E. Peterson and David E. Campbell (Washington, D.C.: Brookings Institution Press, 2001).

vert the nation's shared civic culture by teaching a narrow, intolerant sectarian creed. That is to say, the critics believe that the consequences of school choice are generally and for the most part illiberal and antidemocratic.

The facts tell a different story. Mounting evidence suggests that the appeal of school choice programs is strongest among low-income parents in districts with poorly performing schools, and that the primary reason such parents have for taking advantage of choice does not concern diversity or religion but the opportunity to place their children in schools that will provide a better basic education.[21] The evidence also indicates that charter schools do a better job of providing diversity in the classroom than do regular public schools.[22] In addition, evidence shows that programs that provide cash vouchers do not decrease per-student spending in public schools.[23] Far from weakening public schools, some school choice programs, by creating competition for students, may actually improve public schools.[24] And contrary to warnings issued by academic political theorists (often teaching at elite private universities) that private schools, especially private religious schools, will fail to teach the values and principles crucial to sustaining a pluralistic democracy, studies show that private schools appear to teach political tolerance more effectively than do public schools.[25]

In sum, market-based remedies to the crisis of our public schools seem to be on the side of progress, liberalism, and

21. Terry Moe, "Schools, Vouchers, and the American Public," ibid.
22. "Chester E. Finn Jr., Bruno V. Manno, and Gregg Vanourek, "Charters, Vouchers, and Public Education," ibid.
23. Frederick M. Hess, "Revolution at the Margins," ibid.
24. Ibid.
25. Patrick J. Wolf, Jay P. Greene, Brett Kleitz, and Kristina Thalhammer, "Private Schooling and Political Tolerance," in *Charters, Vouchers, and Public Education.*

democracy, while insistence that the state is the primary solution to the ills that afflict our public schools seems to reflect a misguided attachment to order and the old ways of doing things. Why is it so hard for so many who see themselves as progressives to see this? Why is the left wing of the Democratic Party so hostile to school choice?

IV

The political root of progressive hostility to school choice no doubt can be traced to the Democratic Party's unseemly dependence upon the teachers unions, which except for increased state spending per pupil, and higher salaries and greater benefits for teachers, have never seemed to have seen an educational reform that they have liked.

The intellectual root of the progressive hostility to school choice goes deeper, however, and it can be traced to a homogenizing tendency that arises within the liberal tradition, going back to Locke, and including Montesquieu, Madison, Mill, and many others, of the fundamental moral premise of the natural freedom and equality of all. That tradition underlies our constitutional order, and it links right and left in our politics today. Its homogenizing tendency is not the tradition's only or essential tendency but it is a powerful one. Homogenizing liberalism wants all individuals to be autonomous, free agents who through the exercise of reason have transcended narrow communal and religious attachments and are bound together by their shared capacity for choosing how they shall live. And homogenizing liberalism wants the state to take responsibility for ensuring the achievement of rational autonomy by its citizens, for the state alone has the resources to rescue children from negligent or sectarian parents and, through public education, instill autonomy. The achievement of rational autonomy, the homogenizing liberal believes, is not merely good for the individual but perhaps the highest good and both a benefit and duty of citizenship in a liberal state.

Alas, in pursuing this ambitious educational program, homogenizing liberalism betrays an illiberal impulse and threatens the freedom and dignity of the individual. Even as thoughtful a political theorist and as committed a liberal as Princeton's Stephen Macedo, in the name of autonomy, wants our public schools to form individuals in a single mold. "We have every reason," Macedo writes, "to take seriously the political project of educating future citizens with an eye to their responsibilities as critical interpreters of our shared political traditions—that is, as participants in a democratic project of reason giving and reason demanding."[26] Actually, we have good reason to reject such a state-organized and administered political project. Precisely because of the importance of education to a free citizenry, the task of politics should be to the extent possible to protect public education from politicization. Insisting that the state take responsibility for educating all students in Macedo's mold would be well and good if it were among a liberal state's legitimate aims to raise up a nation of citizen political theorists. Perhaps not incidentally, Macedo's view of education might also have the effect of transforming those who have made political theory their profession into the supreme citizens.

Recently (2003), from a very similar perspective, Macedo's Princeton colleague Amy Gutmann has sought to assess the case for school choice.[27] Gutman declares that "vouchers are

26. Stephen Machedo, *Diversity and Distrust* (Cambridge, Mass.: Harvard University Press, 2001), p. 165.

27. Amy Gutmann, "Assessing Arguments for School Choice: Pluralism, Parental rights, or Education Results," in *School Choice: The Moral Debate*,

both the most celebrated and the most criticized of the new reform ideas for publicly funded schooling in the United States."[28] Her aim is "to carefully examine their promise,"[29] and to discuss the "strongest arguments in favor of vouchers."[30] She concludes that the arguments are generally quite weak. But her assessment is riddled with flaws: it tends to adorn the arguments for school choice with implications and consequences that do not follow, it raises irrelevant and obscurantist objections, and it asserts imperiously but fails to show that the true arguments for vouchers are the most maximal and controversial arguments.

Gutmann addresses first what she calls the argument for school choice from "pluralism." In what proves to be a typical procedure, she cites a snippet from the position of distinguished legal scholar Michael McConnell: "The 'core idea' behind vouchers, McConnell argues, is that 'families [i.e., parents] be permitted to choose among a range of educational options . . . using their fair share of education funding to pay for the schooling they choose.'"[31] To which Gutmann replies, "If this is what pluralism means, then the nonvoucher school system in the United States is certainly pluralistic."[32] She further contends that the demands of the school choice advocates who argue from pluralism have already been met by the system currently in place and therefore vouchers are superfluous. This argument is plain silliness: pluralism is not some sort of fixed quantity of alternatives, but rather a systematic orientation or

---

ed. Alan Wolfe (Princeton, N.J.: Princeton University Press, 2003), pp. 127–48.

28. Gutmann, "Assessing Arguments," p. 127.
29. Ibid.
30. Ibid., p. 128.
31. Ibid.
32. Ibid., p. 129.

openness to new alternatives and experiments. Moreover, it is equally unresponsive to the best pluralist arguments for school choice for Gutmann to complain that the evidence is lacking that the vouchers *promote* pluralism.[33] Put aside for the moment that she does not address the studies that suggest that students in private secular and religious schools actually may develop more pluralistic and participatory dispositions.[34] The fact is that the strongest argument for school choice only requires that vouchers be *consistent* with pluralism, which Gutmann does not deny.

Gutmann's assessment of what she calls the "parental rights" argument is similarly flawed. For starters, she subtly reworks it, substituting an extreme and indefensible version for the balanced and respectable version she actually cites. Another distinguished legal scholar, Charles Fried, argues, according to Gutmann, that, "'the right to form one's child's values, [and] one's child's life plan . . . are extensions of the basic right not to be interfered with in doing these things for oneself.'"[35] To put Fried in his place, Gutmann invokes a few phrases from John Stuart Mill, who in *On Liberty* did deride the view that "'a man's children were supposed to be literally . . . a part of himself,'" and adamantly denied the presumption that parents have a right to "absolute and exclusive control" over their children.[36] Fair enough, but the extreme views Mill condemns are not implied in the fragments from Fried that Gutmann quotes nor does Fried argue for them elsewhere. Notwithstanding Gutmann's obscurantism, the serious moral and constitutional question is not whether parents have rights with

33. See ibid., pp. 129–36.
34. See, e.g., Wolf et al., "Private Schooling and Political Tolerance."
35. Gutmann, pp. 136–37. See also Charles Fried, *Right and Wrong* (Cambridge, Mass.: Harvard University Press, 1998), p. 152.
36. Gutmann, p. 137.

regard to their children. They do. Nor is it whether those rights are absolute. Of course they are not. The question is how far parental rights extend, and where and under what circumstances do the state's right and obligation to ensure that each child receive a basic education clash with parents' right and obligation to educate their children in accordance with their best judgment about what serves their children's best interests.

The argument for school choice in no way depends on the illiberal argument that Gutmann imputes to Fried as the essential argument, that parents' rights over their children are absolute. It does depend on the sensible and decent argument, consistent with liberal principles, that a special relation obtains between parents and children, that parents have both a right and a duty to educate their children, that that right is limited by the purpose of education, which is to enable children when they reach maturity to govern their own lives, that the state has an interest in ensuring that children acquire the basic knowledge and skills they need to maintain themselves as free citizens, that this goal can be achieved in a variety of ways including public and private schooling, and that consequently the state ought to grant parents wide but not unlimited latitude concerning decisions about how their children should be educated. By the way, this more refined liberal position, which indeed supports school choice, is also, contrary to what Gutmann implies, entirely consistent with the extended account of education John Stuart Mill provides in Chapter 5 of *On Liberty*. Indeed, though one would never guess it from the use Gutmann makes of the truncated phrases she adduces from *On Liberty,* Mill clearly believed that the primary responsibility for ensuring the education of children lies with parents.

Gutmann also attacks the strand of the parental rights argument that emphasizes the rights of, or what the state particularly owes, poor parents and their children. She insists that proponents of vouchers who think that poor parents whose children attend woefully deficient public schools should have the same opportunity that rich parents have to send their children to private schools misunderstand the true character of their argument:

> The problem with defending vouchers as a second or third best response on grounds of fairness to poor children is that the inner logic of voucher proposals—and the aim of many proponents—is equal public financing for all parents, regardless of their income and wealth, to pick a private or public school for their children at public expense, not good schooling for all children.[37]

Gutmann is wrong about the inner logic of voucher proposals, and she does not even offer an argument to refute. The fact is that there is no inconsistency in holding that voucher plans are one among many remedies for chronically failing public schools, and that they can be crafted to be consistent with, indeed complemented by, simultaneous efforts to improve public schools.

As were her assessments of the supposed fallacies of the arguments from pluralism and parental rights, so too is her assessment of the fallacies of what she calls the argument from "educational results" defective. She quotes prominent political scientists John E. Chubb and Terry M. Moe as arguing that a voucher plan "has the capacity, *all by itself* to bring about the kind of transformation that, for years, reformers have been seeking to engineer in myriad other ways."[38] But in the very next sentence in her rendition of the argument, she changes it: "Vouchers uniquely have this capacity, advocates say, because competition in a free market is the only way of really improv-

37. Ibid., pp. 139–40.
38. Ibid., p. 140.

ing the quality of just about anything people want in the world, and parents certainly want better schools for their children."[39] This time she does not cite Chubb and Moe or for that matter any of those "advocates" who believe that the market is a remedy to *all* the defects of social life. Perhaps she abandons citation because it interferes with her creation of a strawman. Her rendition certainly is not Chubb and Moe's argument: the claim that a voucher plan can bring about *all* the desired transformations in education is not the same as the claim that *only* a voucher plan can bring about the desired transformations.

The strongest argument from educational results is that since all other remedies have failed, and since the teachers unions have a stranglehold on the bureaucracies that control schools and have given marching orders to the Democratic Party to resist any and all market-based reforms (a political reality about which Gutmann says precisely nothing), injecting market incentives into the system can have a salutary effect. Gutmann notes that so far the data do not show marked improvement in the test scores of the students in voucher plans and do not suggest that "school choice by itself is anything close to a surefire way of improving the education of a sizable proportion of students at risk."[40] But why should voucher plans have to meet a higher standard than public schools? And since when must a remedy for a massive injustice—in this case the quality of inner-city education—be "surefire"? Why is it not enough that the available evidence is that carefully crafted voucher plans can provide a partial remedy for a small proportion of students who are suffering as a result of broken-down public schools?

39. Ibid.
40. Ibid., p. 142.

In the end, even Gutmann is forced to admit that some forms of school choice are defensible and desirable:

> . . . it must also be said that some voucher programs—those which target the children most at risk in inner-city schools— offer long awaited hope for at least some parents. If inner-city public schools do not improve and suburban schools continue to be off-bounds to inner-city parents, it will become politically harder and democratically less defensible to oppose subsidizing private schools that are willing and able to provide a better education on a nondiscriminatory basis to at least some otherwise at-risk students. Some private schools in our inner cities—Catholic schools especially— have demonstrated that they are able to do this for a small but significant number of inner-city students.[41]

What Gutmann does not acknowledge is that the forms of school choice to which, at the end of her article, she grudgingly gives her blessing, and reluctantly allows are consistent with democratic imperatives and constitutional constraints, are precisely the sort of the programs the Court upheld as constitutional in *Zelman*.

It should not be as hard as it has proved to be for liberals such as Macedo and Gutmann to appreciate the liberal imperative in the realm of education to give choice a chance. It is a charm and a strength of our constitutional democracy that it provides for more than a single way of being a good citizen and a good human being. Of course public life depends upon a common culture and shared moral principles. And literacy, toleration, and respect for the rule of law are essential, and should be encouraged by the state, through public education and through some sort of minimum national standards. But there is no good reason to suppose that expanding the range of options available to parents for the education of their children

41. Ibid., pp. 147–48.

will produce a generation less able to govern themselves. Moreover, it needs to be better appreciated that those who care for themselves and their friends and their family, who obey the law, and prefer fly-fishing or stamp-collecting or serving lunch to homeless men and women at a community soup kitchen to spending their evenings and free weekends engaged "as critical interpreters of our shared political traditions" also deserve our respect as good citizens and good human beings. Indeed, our country is large and capacious and tolerant enough to recognize as good citizens and good human beings those who not only do not choose to place critical interpretation of our shared political traditions at the core of their lives, but who believe that there are spheres of life in which the ideal of autonomy has a subordinate role.

We need to resist the homogenizing liberalism that seeks to compress all citizens in a single mold. And we have good grounds, rooted in the liberal tradition, for doing so. For coexisting in the liberal tradition alongside the ambition to homogenize is an aspiration to respect individuals and render public life more secure by blending, in politics as well as in the individual soul, the variety of human goods. And on reflection this blending liberalism does better respect individual liberty and our choices about how to live our lives.

It is, however, a confusing feature of the history of our ideas that in the liberal tradition John Stuart Mill is an outstanding representative of both kinds of liberalism. His *On Liberty* famously evokes the hero of homogenizing liberalism, the autonomous, freely choosing, self-sufficient individual, under no authority save his or her own reason. In the name of autonomy, homogenizing liberalism officially opposes state meddling in an individual's private affairs, except to prevent harm to others. It promotes liberty of thought and discussion as the best of means for forming strong, independent individuals capable of understanding and dealing with the complexities of moral and political life. And it understands individuality as an exalted ideal capable of achievement by only a few extraordinary individuals. In reality, however, the homogenizing liberalism that takes its cue from Mill is often eager to wield the authority of the state to regulate private affairs so as to liberate individuals from the ways of life it deems hidebound, cramped, or fettered, which is to say religion and tradition and hierarchy; it is partial to thought and discussion that presupposes or affirms the good of autonomy; and it seeks to impose the exalted ideal of individuality through state regulation of public education.

But the same Mill also teaches, in *On Liberty* (and throughout his voluminous writings), that the claims of individual liberty must be heard fairly and harmonized with those of society and custom and tradition, both for the good of the individual and for the good of society:

> Unless opinions favourable to democracy and to aristocracy, to property and to equality, to co-operation and to competition, to luxury and to abstinence, to sociality and individuality, to liberty and discipline, and all the other standing antagonisms of practical life, are expressed with equal freedom, and enforced and defended with equal talent and energy, there is no chance of both elements obtaining their due. . . .[42]

Moreover, in *Considerations on Representative Government*, Mill insists that modern constitutional democracy is urgently in need of both a party of order and a party of progress, a conservative party and a progressive party, because each party

---

42. *On Liberty*, in *Essays on Politics and Society*, ed. J. M. Robson (Toronto: University of Toronto Press, 1977), chap. 2, p. 251. See also: *On Liberty*, chap. 2, p. 245; and *Considerations on Representative Government*, in *Essays on Politics and Society*, chap. 2, pp. 383–89.

focuses on an essential interest of the state and each by itself neglects the essential state interest to which the other is devoted.[43] And in essay-length tributes, Mill passionately argued that any free country would benefit enormously, as had England, from both the contributions of Jeremy Bentham, who determinedly if one-sidedly showed the dependence of progressive political reform on the power of the cold, calculating intellect, and of Samuel Taylor Coleridge, who tenaciously though tendentiously taught the wisdom of the heart and the reason of tradition.[44] In so arguing, of course, Mill also displayed the utility and the truth of that blending liberalism that seeks to reconcile opposing moral and political positions and competing human goods.

Mill's account in *On Liberty* of the state's limited but vital role in education also reflects the spirit of blending liberalism.[45] Active involvement of the state was necessary to correct the neglect of "one of the most sacred duties of parents," that of providing one's child with "an education fitting him to perform his part well in life towards others and towards himself."[46] It was "almost a self-evident axiom, that the state should require the education, up to a certain standard, of every human being who is born its citizen."[47] Parents who failed to cultivate the moral and intellectual capacities of their child committed a "moral crime" that obliged the state to step in.[48] Mill did not want the state itself to be in the business of pro-

---

43. *Considerations on Representative Government*, preface, p. 373. See also *On Liberty*, chap. 2, pp. 252–53.

44. "Bentham," and "Coleridge," in *Essays on Ethics, Religion, and Society*, ed. J. M. Robson (Toronto: University of Toronto Press, 1969).

45. This discussion draws on my *Virtue and the Making of Modern Liberalism* (Princeton, N.J.: Princeton University Press, 1991).

46. *On Liberty*, chap. 5, p. 301.

47. Ibid.

48. Ibid., pp. 301–2.

viding a universal education: he feared intractable controversies about the content of the curriculum; and in the event of agreement, he feared a uniform education that cultivated nothing so much as uniformity of opinion. But Mill did want the state to enforce a universal standard of education through the administration of public examinations. Parents would be held legally responsible for ensuring that their children acquired a certain minimum of general knowledge. Payments from the state would be provided to parents who could not otherwise afford basic education for their children. In addition, the state would provide certification through examination in the higher branches of knowledge. To prevent the state from improperly influencing the formation of opinion, such examinations—in particular in the fields of morality, politics, and religion— would be confined to facts and opinions on great intellectual controversies that had been held rather than to the truth or falsity of those opinions.[49] In sum, Mill saw the goal of education as disciplining the mind but not in preparing children for a politically engaged life; he ascribed to the state a variety of obligations in the field of education but he emphatically denied it a monopoly; and he held that the primary duty for the education of children resides with parents.

Given what we now know, and viewed in the light of a blending liberalism, progressives and conservatives alike should welcome further experiments in school choice. Such experiments certainly do not pose a discernible threat to public school education in America. Nearly 90 percent of American children continue to be educated at conventional public schools, and the proportions are unlikely to change significantly anytime soon. Indeed, part of the experiment in school choice should involve new forms of public schools, prominent

49. Ibid., pp. 302–5.

among which are the charter schools already in place. And certainly we should do what we can to improve public schools. Meanwhile, for those in greatest need, for those children of low-income parents who seek an alternative to chronically decrepit inner-city public school education, the preliminary results strongly indicate that choice programs do no harm, and appear to do some good. This finding alone gives good reason for the party of order and the party of progress to work together to give school choice a chance.

PART TWO

Zelman v. Simmons-Harris

Policy Implications

6

The Futu
of Schoo.
Vouchers

Terry M. Moe

Not so long ago, educators and their political allies were loudly proclaiming the death of school vouchers. And on the surface at least, they had a plausible case. Election 2000 saw voters give a decisive thumbs-down to voucher initiatives in California and Michigan. Shortly thereafter, a federal appeals court ruled the Cleveland voucher program unconstitutional. The new Bush administration, facing an evenly split Congress, sacrificed vouchers in order to achieve its larger objective, the No Child Left Behind Act. And while all this was going on, *Phi Delta Kappa*, a leading pro–public school journal, was waving around polling numbers showing that support for vouchers had significantly declined among the American public.

But now the shoe is on the other foot. Vouchers are suddenly on the move again. In its landmark decision, *Zelman v. Simmons-Harris*, the U.S. Supreme Court declared that vouchers for religious schools are constitutional—removing a key legal obstacle to the extension of new voucher programs, giving the concept greater legitimacy and visibility, and lighting a fire under voucher activists around the country. Meantime, there has been a surge of applications for participation in the nation's existing voucher programs—in Milwaukee, Cleveland, and Florida—as well as a spate of new proposals, both for vouchers and for tax credits, in state legislatures. And *Phi Delta Kappa* is no longer crowing about how unpopular vouchers are with the American public, because their own polling numbers have dramatically changed.

What is going on here? And where is all this headed? Anyone who wants a good answer would be wise not to pay much attention to the ups and downs of current events, which are often misleading. Just as critics were wrong to declare vouchers dead on the basis of a few short-term developments, so proponents would be wrong to think the current rush of good news will continue unabated. It won't.

The voucher issue is more than just a current event. It is rooted in the substance of American society—in mediocre schools, in the crisis of inner-city education, in the glaring inequities of class and race, in the structure of American government, in the distribution of political power. The issue is not going to disappear because a few developments in the near term happen to go badly. And it isn't guaranteed total triumph because a few of these developments go well. This is a long-term issue, and understanding it requires a long-term perspective.

The Fundamentals of Voucher Politics

For the past decade (and longer), school vouchers have been the most controversial reform in all of American education. The idea seems simple enough: that the government should expand the choices of parents by providing them with publicly funded grants, or vouchers, that they can apply toward tuition at private schools. Its simplicity, however, is deceptive. The voucher idea, if widely and serious applied, is capable of transforming the entire education system. This is what all the fireworks are about.

Leaders of the voucher movement see the public school system as a stagnant bureaucracy that does not and cannot provide the nation's children with quality education. Vouchers, they claim, would open up a range of new opportunities for these children, generate healthy competition for the public schools, promote higher student achievement, and bring about significant improvements in social equity for the disadvantaged, who are now trapped in our nation's worst schools and desperately in need of choice.

Opponents see things very differently. In their view, the public schools are doing a reasonable job despite the burdens under which they operate, and they deserve more political support rather than less. The real effect of vouchers, opponents argue, would be to wreck the public schools by draining off resources and children. In the process, vouchers would undermine cherished values the public school system has long stood for—common schooling, equal opportunity, democratic control—and create a system driven by private interests.

Both sides believe their own arguments and see themselves as fighting for noble causes. This in itself is enough to fuel political conflict. Yet ideas and values alone cannot account for the explosive intensity of the voucher issue in American politics. There is something else going on, something that profoundly shapes the politics of this issue—and can hardly be described as noble.

The public school system as it currently exists is a huge reservoir of money, power, jobs, and patronage. It spends in the range of $400 billion every year, it employs millions of people, and it confers tremendous power on those who control the money and the jobs. Vouchers would affect all this, possibly in very big ways: for when kids use vouchers to go private, money and jobs go with them, and so ultimately does power. For these reasons, the groups that run and materially benefit from the existing system find the voucher issue deeply threatening to their most fundamental interests. And not surprisingly, they are dedicated to opposing it with all the power they can muster.

These established groups are at the forefront of the battle against vouchers. Their undisputed leaders are the teachers unions, which, by virtue of their iron grip over the public schools, have amassed vast economic and organizational resources and huge memberships, and have emerged as perhaps the most powerful interest groups in American politics. For the teachers unions especially, vouchers are a nightmare in the making. Vouchers would lower the number of teachers employed in the public sector, and thus reduce union membership and resources; increase the number of teachers employed in the private sector, where they would be much more difficult to organize for collective bargaining; increase competition among schools, putting union-run schools (which are higher in cost and more bureaucratic) at a disadvantage; and create a more decentralized, less regulated system in which the unions have far less power and control.

When vouchers are being debated in state and national politics, the teachers unions are very adept at talking the talk. They argue in the loftiest language that vouchers would be bad for children or won't really improve the quality of education. But the fact is, these sorts of arguments have little to do with their opposition. If it could be shown beyond a shadow of a doubt that vouchers *are* good for kids and *do* improve the quality of education, the teachers unions would still be vehemently opposed and willing to do anything to stop them. Vouchers threaten their most basic self-interests—including their very survival.

The teachers unions are not alone in opposing vouchers, of course. They are the ones spending the big money, mobilizing the troops, and directing the charge, but they also have important allies in the broader liberal coalition that add force and legitimacy to the war effort. Much of this liberal opposition—unlike the unions' own opposition—derives from a genuine concern for basic principles, values, and deserving constituencies. The NAACP, for instance, fears that vouchers would promote segregation. The ACLU and the People for the American Way are concerned about the separation of church and state. And liberals in general tend to be supportive of government and the public schools, suspicious of markets, and worried that a shift toward choice would hurt the poor.

Even among the more principled liberal opponents, however, self-interest sometimes plays an important role. Some of these organizations, for instance, receive crucial funding from the teachers unions; and they know that, in order to keep it, they cannot defect on the voucher issue. To take another example: many middle class members of the NAACP and other civil rights groups are employees of the public schools system, which has become a major ladder of social advancement for minority groups. These people have a self-interest in opposing vouchers (and other fundamental reforms) purely because their jobs and powers are at stake.

Self-interest also has a lot to do with why most Democratic politicians are so stridently opposed to vouchers. The Democrats are acutely sensitive to the unions' clout in national, state, and local elections, which is second to that of no other interest group. In part, this clout is due to the enormous amounts of money the teachers unions spend on political campaigns. In many states, they are the number one spenders. But the key to their electoral strength is that they literally have millions of members, and these members are a looming presence in *every* electoral district in the country, allowing the unions to mobilize a vast array of organized activities—from phoning to leafletting to pounding the pavement—so crucial to ensuring that friends are elected and enemies defeated. Nationwide, almost all of this weaponry is enlisted in support of Democrats rather than Republicans. But the Democrats don't get it for nothing. They earn the unions' much-valued support by toeing the line on important educational issues. And the one issue they absolutely must toe the line on is vouchers. For now, the Democrats are simply in the unions' pocket on this issue. They do what the unions say.

The voucher coalition is a wholly different phenomenon. It is a political movement and, like most movements, it is far less organized than the defenders of the existing system, has fewer resources, and has no institutional base. Self-interest clearly has something to do with its power, but it is a self-interest that seems entirely appropriate and socially desirable—namely, the self-interest of parents who want better schools for their kids. This interest is especially strong among parents who are dissatisfied with their public schools, particularly parents who are poor, minority, and stuck in failing urban school districts. In politics, however, the masses of rank-and-file parents are extremely difficult to organize, and usually play little direct role. There are other constituencies that might be construed as having a self-interested stake in the voucher issue: private schools, for example, and churches. But the fact is, leaders of these groups have usually not been at the forefront of the movement.

The people carrying the cause forward are essentially activists—most of them conservatives, a growing number of them advocates for the poor—who see vouchers as socially beneficial and have no self-interested stake in it. Even the people who have contributed major sums of money—John Walton and Theodore Forstmann, for instance, who recently contributed $100 million of their own money to fund private voucher programs—have done so because they believe in the cause, and not because they have anything to gain from it materially. There are some Republican officials who have electoral incentives (and thus self-interested incentives) to support vouchers, because they may come from districts in which vouchers are popular. But most Republicans have constituencies in the suburbs, where the schools are okay and vouchers are not a searing issue. The strongest support for vouchers comes from parents in the worst districts—and these districts tend not to be Republican. Thus, when Republicans support vouchers, it is often for reasons of ideology and personal belief, not simple self-interest. The Democrats are much more dedicated to the defeat of vouchers than Republicans are to their adoption.

Any effort to gain perspective on the voucher issue, therefore, must recognize that this is an issue that enters the political arena at a profound disadvantage. It faces an enemy that is one of the most powerful interest groups in the country, sees the issue as a mortal threat, and is totally committed to its defeat. That enemy is supported by a broader coalition that adds considerable power to the effort—and includes an army of Democratic officials who, in occupying pivotal positions of public authority, can be counted upon to protect the unions' vested interests and close ranks whenever the voucher issue comes up.

This combination is tough to beat. In the grander scheme of things, it is simply one illustration of why institutional systems everywhere, not just in education and not just in the United States, are so supremely stable and difficult to change: all systems generate vested interests, and the vested interests

use their considerable power—derived from the system itself—
to maintain existing arrangements and prevent change. Almost
all the time, the vested interests win. Regardless of the merits.
And almost all the time, the people who challenge the system
in a serious way can expect to get their heads handed to them.

While this is a universal axiom of politics, it is true in
spades in this country. We have something extra that magnifies
the power of vested interests still further and makes the status
quo even more difficult to change. What is this something
extra? It is simply the familiar structure of American government. Beginning some two hundred years ago and continuing
to the present day, our democratic institutions have been
designed via myriad checks and balances to make the passage
of new laws very difficult and to make blocking very easy. In
the usual policymaking process, advocates for any change in
the status quo (such as a voucher program) must successfully
make it past *all* the hurdles that stand in their way—subcom-
mittees, full committees, and floor votes in two houses of the
legislature, plus executive vetoes, court decisions, and more—
while the opponents simply have to win at any *one* of these
points to block. Thus, the opponents of change have a huge
structural advantage. Even if they command little public or
elite support, they can often find a veto point at some stage of
the game that will stop the proposed change from going forward. And if the opponents are politically powerful—as the
teachers unions and their allies surely are—then it is virtually
guaranteed that they can do so.

These are the fundamentals of voucher politics, and they
aren't pretty. The movement is doubly disadvantaged. In the
first place, raw power is heavily stacked against it. In the second place, the political battle is being fought out within a governmental structure that favors opponents, and that skews the
power imbalance even further. Given this context, it follows

that the voucher movement is sure to generate a great many political losses in its quest to change American education, at least in the early years (such as now) when the opponents are at their most powerful. Losses have to be considered normal, and an entirely necessary part of the process of change. Progress must come through small victories, usually won at rare times and places when the political stars happen to line up just right.

Initiative Politics

Voucher advocates are well aware that power is stacked against them, and that the checks and balances of American government make the prospects for change even worse. In the short term, they know they cannot do much about union power. But they have occasionally sought to improve their chances of success—and indeed, to score big, dramatic victories—by circumventing the structural disadvantages that American government places upon them. This they have done by taking their case directly to the people through the initiative process, which in twenty-four states offers an alternative arena in which policies can get adopted.

Theoretically, this is a terrific idea. But in practice it doesn't work. Over the past decade, vouchers (or tuition tax credits) have been put before the voters seven times, and in each case they have been defeated by big margins. The defeats in California and Michigan are just the most recent in a long line of electoral failures.

Losing at the ballot box creates obvious problems for the movement, because it gives opponents ammunition for saying that the American people, when given a choice, simply do not want vouchers. The 2000 election returns were barely counted before Robert Chase, president of the National Education Association, was proclaiming that "The resounding defeat of vouchers in Michigan and California should put an end to the myth that voters want vouchers. . . . This thorough thrashing of vouchers should be the death knell to a bad idea."

The real reason that vouchers have gone down so badly in these initiative campaigns has little to do, however, with the meaningful expression of public opinion. While it might seem that direct democracy should offer the purest possible measure of the general will, there is a perverse logic that drives the dynamics of these elections. This logic almost guarantees that vouchers cannot win, regardless of how sympathetic people might be toward the idea from the outset. Here is why.

There is a good deal of independent research on initiative campaigns, ranging across all types of policy issues, and it shows pretty clearly that, unless the issue is familiar to voters and fairly simple for them to evaluate—as is the case, for instance, with the death penalty, assisted suicide, gambling, and many others—a strong opponent (if there is one) can almost always defeat it, often by big margins. This happens not because the issue is unpopular. Indeed, the very popularity of the issue as measured by pre-election polls and focus groups is usually what convinces proponents to put the issue on the ballot in the first place. Defeat is in the cards because, with an unfamiliar and rather complicated issue, a well-heeled opponent can unleash a media campaign—filled with extreme claims, half-truths, and even outright lies—that generates doubt and uncertainty among many voters and causes them to fall back on the status quo (even if they don't like it much). The maxim among voters in these situations is "when in doubt, vote no." Big spending by the initiative's advocates cannot stop this hemorrhage of support from occurring. Nor does it much matter if the initiative is well designed. A well-financed opponent is going to win.

The voucher issue is surely in this category. Many polls have shown that the American people are basically open to the idea. A 1999 survey by Public Agenda, for instance, showed that 57 percent expressed support for vouchers, with 36 percent opposed. (The figures for parents were 68 percent in support and 27 percent opposed) This same survey, however, also showed that some two-thirds of the public had little familiarity with the issue. So at least for now, it fails the familiarity test. It also fails the simplicity test. For there are obviously many dimensions to its possible social effects—on school quality, social equity, racial balance, costs, taxes, accountability, the separation of church and state—that make it inherently complicated. Under these conditions, an opponent can have a field day with its media campaign. Vouchers would ruin the public schools. Vouchers would raise taxes. Private schools would discriminate against the poor. Ideologues and religious cults would propagandize children. And so on. These sorts of sensational charges can be carefully and thoroughly rebutted by voucher advocates, but not in the midst of a full-blown media war, where the potential for voter education and considered judgment is near zero. The opponent wins.

So electoral defeats do not mean that the voucher idea is unpopular. There is, however, an essential feature of public opinion that is surely finding expression in these election results, and that gives opponents something extra to work with in sowing the seeds of doubt and uncertainty. This is an important part of the political equation and needs underlining.

The fact is, despite all the concern among policymakers about improving education, most Americans very much like the public school system. They tend to think their local schools are performing reasonably well. They also believe in the ideals of public education: they see it as a pillar of democracy and the local community, they admire the egalitarian principles on which it is based, and they think it deserves our commitment and support. They embrace what I call the "public school ideology."

Although most Americans are not paying attention to the nation's voucher debate, their basic values put them on both sides of the fence at once. They are open to the idea of vouchers, think private schools are superior to public schools, and believe it makes sense to give new opportunities to children who need them. Yet they also have a genuine attachment to the public school system, and this attachment makes them wary of any reforms that might seem to threaten the schools' well-being. They are sitting ducks, as a result, for a campaign that makes sensational claims about the frightening risks of vouchers, and this is one reason the opponents find it so easy to win.

Voucher advocates can rightly complain that public opinion is being manipulated in these situations. But the manipulation is also rooted in something very real that cannot help but shape the movement's strategies and prospects more generally. Americans are not interested in revolution. They want to keep the public system, make it better, and perhaps add vouchers. But only if the risks to the public schools can be kept to a minimum.

Legislative Politics

For the foreseeable future, the voucher movement cannot use initiative campaigns to get around the checks and balances that the American political system places in its way. As most of its leaders now realize, the movement has little choice but to pour its energies and resources into the usual policymaking process, and thus to pursue its aims by getting legislatures to pass new laws, getting executives to sign them, and getting the courts to uphold them. The process being what it is, and opponents being as strong as they are, progress can only come through incremental, hard-won steps that bring about change over a long period of time. But the key question is: can serious progress really be made at all, or are the barriers to success simply prohibitive?

The outlook is surprisingly positive. The barriers to success are largely beyond the movement's control, but not entirely. There are things the movement can do to improve its prospects considerably, and thus to win small victories more often than it otherwise would. Notably, it can move to the political center—by making moderate, low-risk proposals for change and, on that basis, putting together diverse coalitions that reach across ideological lines. In the short run, moderate proposals and diverse coalitions can win battles here and there. In the long run, they can break down the liberal coalition and leave the teachers unions virtually alone and unable to hold back the tide. These developments are more than abstractions. They are already under way.

For decades after Milton Friedman first introduced the voucher idea, the budding choice movement was essentially a conservative phenomenon, driven by the ideals of people who firmly believed in the power of markets to improve the schools. The connection between choice and conservatism made good sense and was crucial to the movement's emergence as a political force. Nonetheless, conservatism alone was too narrow a political base—not moderate enough, not diverse enough—to overcome the blocking power of the established interests. If the movement wanted to bring about change, it first had to change itself.

The spark came in 1990, through an event that may someday be regarded as one of the most significant developments in the history of American education. Certainly it is the single most critical event in the struggle for school choice. What happened was that inner-city parents, organized and led by local activists—most notably, Polly Williams—rose up to demand vouchers as a means of escape from their failing public schools. And by entering into a coalition with conservatives—led by Republican Governor Tommy Thompson—the urban poor won a surprising victory over the powerful defenders of the existing system. The result was the nation's first public voucher program: a small pilot program reserved (at the time) for no more than 1,000 disadvantaged children in inner-city Milwaukee. But the victory did more than put vouchers on the map. It also generated a dramatic change in the guiding ideals and internal makeup of the voucher movement as a whole, and set the "new" movement on a very different and far more promising path.

Since 1990, most of the movement's efforts have focused on providing vouchers to poor and minority families in the inner cities: families that are concentrated in low-performing schools and trapped by the searing inequities of the current system. The new arguments for vouchers have less to do with free markets than with social equity. And they have less to do with theory than with the commonsense notions that disadvantaged kids should be given immediate opportunities to get out of bad schools, and that experiments, pilot programs, and novel approaches are good ideas in urban systems that are clearly failing, and for which the downside risk is virtually nil.

This shift has put the opponents of vouchers in an extremely awkward position. As liberals, they claim to be (and usually are) champions of the poor. But on the voucher issue, they flatly refuse to represent their own constituents—and indeed, find themselves fighting *against* poor families, who are only trying to escape conditions that liberals agree are deplorable. In doing so, moreover, liberals have essentially pushed the urban poor into an educational alliance with conservatives. And this alliance, whose arguments for equity, practicality, and low risk have a much broader public appeal than the conservative mantra of free markets, is sometimes powerful enough to bring about political victory, even in a context heavily stacked against it.

This is the alliance that won in Milwaukee. It won again in creating the nation's second voucher program in Cleveland (1995), in vastly expanding the Milwaukee program (1995), and in creating the first state-level voucher program in Florida (1999). And it came close—which is saying a lot, under the circumstances—in many state legislatures, as well as in the federal government (where Congress passed a low-income program for Washington, D.C., only to have it vetoed by President Clinton). Spurred on by the recent Supreme Court decision, these attempts will continue. And some of them will surely succeed.

Outside of politics, this same alliance has also been responsible for creating a vast system of privately funded voucher programs: programs that opponents are powerless to block, and have put vouchers in the hands of more than 70,000 disadvantaged children—far more than in the hotly contested public voucher programs. Because of these private programs, especially, vouchers are increasingly becoming part of the everyday lives of poor families and the everyday experiences of urban communities. People are telling their friends and neighbors, policymakers and other elites are watching and listening. The sociology of the issue is changing.

And there is more. The voucher movement has recently hit upon two promising new avenues for extending the reach of choice. The first follows the lead of Florida, which in 2000 adopted a voucher program that makes every child in special education—some 350,000 of them—eligible for a voucher.

Here too, the focus is on a population of needy children who in many cases are not being well served by the public schools. Here too, it is politically awkward and embarrassing for opponents to argue against. And the numbers are huge—already, in just the second year of the program, about 9,000 special education children are expected to use vouchers to attend private schools, and in future years this figure could increase astronomically.

The second strategy involves tax credits. Over the years, this idea has taken various forms, most often that of giving parents tax credits to compensate them for private school tuition (and perhaps books, transportation, and other expenses). A few states, such as Minnesota and Illinois, have adopted such measures. The more recent development, however—a development with spectacular growth potential for the voucher movement—is the idea that business firms should be given tax credits for allocating money toward specially constituted scholarship foundations, which would then distribute vouchers to qualified children on the basis of need. Pennsylvania and Florida have already adopted such programs; and business firms, often preferring to earmark their money for deserving education programs rather than see it dumped into the general fund, have responded by pouring many millions of dollars into their states' scholarship funds. In 2002–2003, thousands of kids in both states will be attending private schools with the help of these vouchers. And this is just the beginning

Looking Ahead

The teachers unions would like to believe that they can stop these developments, and in the short term there is no doubt that they will win most of the battles. All they want to do is block, and the structure of American politics ensures that they can succeed most of the time. Their prospects over the long haul, however, are another matter—for their political position and ability to block are likely to deteriorate steadily over time. There are three reasons for this.

The first is that the voucher movement benefits from the law of large numbers. There are 15,000 school districts, hundreds of cities, fifty states, and a national government, and all of them are political arenas in which the voucher issue can be fought out. Because the movement itself is fragmented and decentralized, it is guaranteed to generate a great many battles in the years ahead. For a while, almost all these battles will be lost. But with so much action taking place in arenas all over the country, and with the movement taking advantage of windows of opportunity—legislatures controlled by Republicans, districts in crisis, new leaders emerging to represent urban parents—the law of large numbers ensures that it will win some of these battles, even if the probability of victory is small overall. These victories will accumulate over time. And as they do, the unions will suffer losses of members and resources—and become incrementally weaker. Which will increase the probability of voucher victories in future battles. And so it will go.

The second is that, as vouchers are provided to many thousands of kids throughout the country, the social context cannot help but change. I mentioned this earlier with regard to private voucher programs. But it is clearly a consequence as well of all the various public voucher programs, which, while currently small by comparison, are destined to grow tremendously, if only because the programs for special education and the programs financed by business tax credits have the potential to extend vouchers to vast numbers of families. As this happens, vouchers will become a normal part of educational life in America, especially urban America: the home of Dem-

ocratic opponents. No longer will vouchers be regarded as an
alien concept. No longer will opponents be able to claim that
vouchers destroy the public schools—because people will be
able to look around and see that nothing of the sort has happened. Increasingly, vouchers will move from the abstract to
the socially concrete. Many people will benefit from them,
have a stake in them, know friends and relatives who use and
like them, and expect their political representatives to support
them.

Third, as these observations about the social context begin
to suggest, the liberal coalition at the elite level is destined to
break down over time. The key development—which could
happen within five years, but could take a decade or more—is
that the NAACP and other civil rights groups will come to support vouchers for the disadvantaged. Such a claim may seem
fanciful, because these groups have been vociferous in their
opposition thus far. Yet this stance has created serious problems for them: for their own constituents are the ones who are
trapped in our nation's worst schools, and these same constituents are the nation's strongest supporters of vouchers. The
leaders are dramatically out of step with their "followers."

So far they have shown little sign of shifting course. Most
of these leaders have been around since the early years of the
civil rights movement, and they have emerged with a firm set
of convictions—that government is the key to social progress,
that markets don't work for the poor, that choice is simply an
excuse for whites to engage in segregation. Younger blacks,
however, have had very different formative experiences, and
they are much more inclined to see choice as a means of
empowering minorities and promoting equity and opportunity. These leaders-in-waiting are causing trouble in the lower
ranks of the civil rights groups. And if the current generation
of leaders doesn't come around to vouchers on its own, the

shift will take place when the new generation comes to power. In the meantime, new groups are emerging—notably the Black Alliance for Educational Options, led by Milwaukee's Howard Fuller—dedicated to the empowerment of black families through educational choice. Their claim: that the civil rights groups are out of step with black constituents. This is another reason for the civil rights groups to open up to vouchers. Competitors are moving in to represent the unrepresented.

Civil rights groups will not be the only ones to abandon the teachers unions. The most visible sign of things to come is that certain high-profile liberals have begun to peel off and announce their support for targeted voucher plans. In recent years, the converts include: the *New Republic*, the *Washington Post*, former secretary of labor Robert Reich (when he's not running for governor), civil rights activist Andrew Young, and former secretary of health, education, and welfare Joseph Califano. Their support for vouchers arises out of liberal principles and concerns. They don't rave about free markets. They see vouchers as an experimental but sensible means of providing much-needed assistance to disadvantaged kids, and of trying to shake up a status quo that, in many urban areas, is demonstrably inequitable and resistant to change.

There is evidence, then, that the opponents of vouchers are beginning to lose the intellectual and moral arguments within their own coalition. Important as this is, however, it will take more than the force of ideas to convince most Democratic officeholders to turn against the teachers unions too. The unions have always been able to rely on the Democrats to keep voucher plans from passing into law, and there is little mystery why. Sheer power keeps them in line. Still, this era of lockstep Democratic compliance cannot last. Many Democrats, like the civil rights groups, find their opposition acutely uncomfortable: they have constituents who are disadvantaged, in bad schools, and strongly interested in vouchers. At the mass level, in fact, vouchers could very easily be a Democratic issue—but Democratic politicians have not been able to treat it that way. Were it not for the unions, many Democrats, especially those representing inner-city areas, would simply line up with their own constituents.

Eventually, this is what will happen. The shift to vouchers by prominent liberals will help pave the way, making it easier for some Democrats to justify their defection. But the union grip will really start to loosen when the civil rights groups begin to make the switch themselves. This will change the balance of raw political power, and with it the incentives of Democratic politicians to vote their constituencies. Increasingly, the unions will be left alone, out on the extreme.

These changes may take decades to be realized. The new system that evolves, moreover, will fall well short of what some of the purists in the choice movement might want. Free markets will not reign, the public system will not be privatized, and vouchers may never be extended to all kids on a universal basis. Given the checks and balances inherent in American government, the changes that actually come about will tend to be those that the new and future recruits to vouchers—urban activists, civil rights groups, prominent liberals, urban Democrats—are willing to go along with. They are the ones who hold the balance of power, and they will be using that power to aid the disadvantaged, promote social equity, and ensure that government continues to play an important role in education.

Vouchers are not the only choice-based reforms that we can expect. For similar reasons, there will also be thousands of new charter schools offering choice and competition within the public system. And there will be lots of innovative contracting arrangements, in which private firms (such as Edison) are engaged to run schools. The new system will be a blend of all these (and more), and is best thought of as a mixed system of government and markets—a system that involves far more choice, competition, and privatization than the current system does, but maintains a key role for government in helping ensure that these market forces work as desired and that key social values—especially equity for the disadvantaged—are protected and promoted.

Had the Supreme Court prohibited vouchers for religious schools, these developments would have been slowed but not stopped. The socioeconomic fundamentals driving the politics of reform would have stayed the same, after all. And it is likely that advocates would have found other means of extending vouchers to kids in religious schools—for example, appropriately designed tax credits and scholarship foundations—that would have circumvented the Court's decisions, and indeed have gained explicit Court approval.

As it is, a favorable Supreme Court decision has removed a key legal obstacle to change, and the socioeconomic and political forces I've described can work their influence more quickly and effectively. Even so, real change will hardly come overnight. It will take a long time—twenty years, thirty years, perhaps more—for the system to be thoroughly transformed. In the meantime, vouchers will continue to have their ups and downs, and we simply have to see them for what they are: short-term fluctuations in a long-term process of change.

7

The Future
of Tax
Credits

MARTIN R. WEST

The turmoil surrounding school vouchers has led some law-makers in recent years to seek out alternative means of enhancing private school choice. Derided by critics as "stealth vouchers," proposals for tax deductions and credits for private school tuition have nonetheless met with considerable political success. By the close of 2002, six states were offering tax relief for families paying private school tuition or making donations to private scholarship organizations. Each of these programs was established or significantly expanded since 1997, during which time more than twenty other states and the U.S. Congress had considered similar proposals.[1]

This flurry of legislative activity raises many questions. Where did the idea of tuition tax credits for elementary and secondary education originate, and what accounts for its recent success? Are the programs currently in place harbingers of a comprehensive federal tax credit, is the more likely course of events a gradual proliferation of state-level programs, or will

1. ECS Policy Brief, "School Choice: State Actions," Education Commission of the States, updated May 2002.

this idea wither away? What will be the impact of the Supreme
Court's decision in *Zelman v. Simmons-Harris*, upholding the
constitutionality of Cleveland's voucher program?

At first glance, the distinction between tuition tax credits
and vouchers would appear to be as meaningless as the difference between McDonald's and Burger King. Tax expenditures—or departures from the normal tax structure favoring an
activity, industry, or group—are conceptually equivalent to
direct government spending.[2] Tuition tax credits and vouchers
also face the same political opponents, most notably teachers
unions and other public-school supporters. With considerable
resources at their disposal and a clear incentive to resist
increased competition, these organizations are a potent adver-
sary for any policy that would reduce the cost of private education—even via the relatively discreet vehicle of the tax code.

Yet the apparent similarity between vouchers and tax credits for private school tuition masks important political and
legal differences. For example, tuition tax credits are more
popular than vouchers with the American public. When similar questions about tuition tax credits and vouchers are
included on the same survey, tax credits generate higher levels
of support.[3] The differences, which in recent polls range from

2. Such departures take a variety of forms. Tax credits provide a direct
reduction in an individual's tax liability; a tax deduction is a reduction in
taxable income made prior to the calculation of tax liability. Refundable tax
credits provide individuals whose tax liabilities are less than the value of the
credit with a direct cash payment. The normal tax structure used as a baseline
includes existing tax rates, the personal exemption, the standard deduction,
and the exemption of costs incurred to generate income. Stanley S. Surrey
and Paul R. MacDonald, *Tax Expenditures* (Cambridge, Mass.: Harvard University Press, 1985).

3. For the most recent polls with questions about tuition tax credits and
vouchers, see: Lowell C. Rose and Alec M. Gallup, *The 30th Annual Phi Delta
Kappa/Gallup Poll of the Public's Attitudes Toward the Public Schools* (Phi
Delta Kappa International, 1998); Lowell C. Rose and Alec M. Gallup, *The*

8 to 14 percentage points, may reflect Americans' skepticism regarding direct government spending. Alternatively, they may reflect the fact that tuition tax credits have been spared some of the negative media coverage vouchers have received. Regardless, the pattern suggests that tuition tax credits have enjoyed at least a temporary political advantage over vouchers.

Tuition tax credits also offer lawmakers greater flexibility in program design than do vouchers. Arizona, Florida, and Pennsylvania, for example, all now offer tax credits not to tuition-paying parents but rather to individuals or corporations making donations to organizations granting scholarships for private education. By expanding the segment of the population with a stake in the policy, this approach has the potential to increase support for school choice beyond the subset of parents with a desire to move their children to private schools.

Finally, tuition tax credits have an important legal advantage over vouchers in many states. *Zelman* notwithstanding, doubts about the acceptability of vouchers continue to hinder their enactment in the majority of U.S. states whose constitutions contain more restrictive language regarding the separation of church and state. Tuition tax credits, which have generally not been construed as "public money," largely avoid this concern.

But until recently these advantages had not been sufficient to yield legislative success. As the following section documents, Congress has considered proposals to use the federal tax code to compensate families for tuition expenses intermittently for more than three decades. Originally devised as a strategy to aid struggling private schools, these proposals have

---

31st Annual Phi Delta Kappa/Gallup Poll of the Public's Attitudes Toward the Public Schools (Phi Delta Kappa International, 1999).

consistently failed to gain enough support to become law.[4] Congressional debates over tuition tax credits underscore a persistent obstacle confronting any school choice proposal at the federal level—their budgetary impact. The federal government spends so little on public education that financial support for private school choice inevitably amounts to substantial expenditure with little in the way of potential savings, suggesting the prospects for the expansion of school choice are most favorable in the states.

Federal Tuition Tax Credits: A Political History

Origins

The tax credit movement took off in the early 1970s in response to a fiscal crisis afflicting the nation's private schools. Foremost among the causes were the increasing cost of teachers' labor and steady reductions in class size in the public sector, with which private schools competed for students.[5] The problem of rising costs was aggravated for the Catholic schools that served more than 80 percent of all private school students by a decline in the number of nuns and priests serving as teachers.[6] With

4. An exception that proves the rule was the tentative expansion of Coverdell Education Savings Accounts in 2001 to include elementary and secondary school tuition expenses. H.R. 1836, P.L. 107–16.

5. For trends in teachers' wages and class size, and a discussion of the relationship between them, see Darius Lakdawalla, "Quantity Over Quality," *Education Next* 2, no. 3 (Fall 2002): 67–72. For trends in per-pupil spending, see Eric A. Hanushek, "School Resources and Student Performance," in Gary Burtless, ed., *Does Money Matter? The Effect of School Resources on Student Achievement and Adult Success* (Washington, D.C.: Brookings Institution Press, 2002), pp. 43–73.

6. Statement of the National Catholic Educational Association, U.S. Congress, United States Senate, Subcommittee on Education of the Committee on Labor and Public Welfare, *Hearings on Aid to Nonpublic Education*, 92d Congress, 2d sess., December 2, 1971, and January 11, 1972, p. 258.

no relief from these pressures in sight, many observers concluded that the days of a robust Catholic school system were "numbered."[7]

President Nixon's initial response to what he described as the "potential collapse" of the private sector was to designate a panel within the President's Commission on School Finance to study the problems of nonpublic schools. Nixon offered Congress a long list of reasons to justify his concern, claiming that private schools "give a spur of competition to the public schools," "give parents the opportunity to send their children to a school of their own choice and of their own religious denomination," increase "experimentation," and create "special opportunities for minorities." He placed particular emphasis on the dire fiscal consequences should the nonpublic sector be allowed to collapse. "If most or all private schools were to close or turn public," he said, "the added burden on public funds by the end of the 1970s would exceed $4 billion per year on operations, with an estimated $5 billion more needed for facilities."[8]

Eighteen months later Nixon reiterated his concern, this time before an enthusiastic audience of 1,500 Catholics gathered at a Knights of Columbus dinner: "At a time when we see those private and parochial schools . . . closing at the rate of one a day, we must resolve to stop that trend and turn it around. You can count on my support to do that."[9] Quite

7. "Catholic Schools: Their Days May be Numbered," *New York Times*, November 28, 1971.

8. Richard Nixon, "Education for the 1970s, Renewal and Reform." Reprinted in *Hearings on Aid to Nonpublic Education*, p. 62.

9. Richard Nixon, "The President's Remarks to the 89th Annual International Meeting of the Knights of Columbus in New York City," *Weekly Compilation of Presidential Documents, August 23, 1971*, p. 1179. For media coverage of the address, see "Nixon Vows to Help Parochial Schools; Cardinal Calls Government Aid a Right," *New York Times*, August 18, 1971.

clearly Nixon saw the issue as one popular with a pivotal group of voters in the period leading up to the 1972 election.

Many prominent Democrats shared the Nixon administration's interest in the continued viability of private education. In late 1971, for example, the Senate Committee on Labor and Public Welfare's Subcommittee on Education, chaired by Democratic Senator Claiborne Pell of Rhode Island, held a series of public hearings to devise strategies to allocate government funds to private schools.

Any proposal Pell's committee devised would inevitably raise doubts regarding its constitutionality. In June of 1971 the Supreme Court in *Lemon v. Kurtzman* struck down a Pennsylvania statute that reimbursed private and parochial schools for the cost of providing education in secular subjects. The *Lemon* decision established a more stringent constitutional standard to be applied to statutes providing aid to religious schools. Previous decisions had relied exclusively on the "purpose test" (does the statute reflect a legitimate secular purpose?) and the "primary effect test" (is the primary effect of the statute to advance or inhibit religion?). Without dismissing these guidelines, the *Lemon* court added a third that asked whether the administration of the statute would lead to "excessive entanglement" of government with religion. The Pennsylvania statute failed this test by requiring that the state monitor instruction in religious schools to ensure that it was conducted in accordance with statutory restrictions.

The court's reasoning in *Lemon* created something of a dilemma for those seeking to channel government funds into failing private schools. As Stephen Kurzman of the Department of Health, Education, and Welfare explained to Pell and his committee:

[T]he government may not, in giving assistance to sectarian schools, permit that assistance to be used to promote religion. But if the government takes steps to see to it that the assistance is not used for that purpose, the government is likely to become "excessively," and therefore unconstitutionally, "entangled" with religion.[10]

The fact that tax credits did not involve actual government expenditures minimized constitutional concerns. In fact, the same criteria applied to strike down the Pennsylvania tuition reimbursement program in *Lemon* had been fashioned in a 1970 ruling *upholding* the constitutionality of property tax exemptions for religious institutions in New York.[11] It was therefore predictable that Nixon's special Panel on Nonpublic Education would include among its recommendations, issued on April 14, 1972, the "prompt enactment by Congress of legislation to authorize Federal income tax credit to parents for part of tuition payments to nonpublic elementary and secondary schools."[12]

Despite the panel's report, it was not until 1976 that a measure offering direct tax relief for private school parents received a floor vote in either chamber of Congress. In that year,

10. Statement of Assistant Secretary for Legislation Stephen Kurzman, *Hearings on Aid to Nonpublic Education*, p. 13. The severity of this constraint should not be overstated; the Supreme Court had previously found constitutional a variety of government programs providing financial assistance to religious schools for legitimate secular purposes, such as the transportation of pupils and the purchase of textbooks. Yet discussions in both Congress and the media indicate that there was a great deal of uncertainty about what was currently permissible and how precedent was likely to evolve in the future.

11. *Walz v. Tax Commission of New York*, 397 U.S. 664 (1970).

12. The President's Panel on Nonpublic Education, *Nonpublic Education and the Public Good*, April 1972. Reprinted in U.S. Congress, House of Representatives, Committee on Ways and Means, *Hearings on Tax Credits for Nonpublic Education*, 92d Congress, 2d sess., August 1972, pp. 107–71.

Senator James Buckley, a Catholic Republican from New York initially elected as a member of the Conservative Party, offered a floor amendment to the 1976 Tax Reform Bill that would have made all taxpayers eligible for a modest tax credit of up to $1,000 annually for tuition payments to institutions of higher education, vocational schools, and elementary and secondary schools. The measure was defeated by a 52–37 vote, with Republicans voting 18–16 in favor, and Democrats 19–36 opposed.[13] Although unsuccessful, Buckley's proposal set the stage for a more extended debate just two years later.

1978: Victory in the House

The 1978 struggle over tax credits for elementary and secondary school tuition began as part of a broader debate over similar credits for higher education. Like most tax measures, discussion of tuition tax credits began in the House Ways and Means Committee. Arguments for including elementary and secondary school tuition expenses centered on the still precarious financial situation of private and parochial schools. Organizations representing these schools lobbied extensively on the Hill and committee members from heavily Catholic districts were inundated with mail from constituents. Three such members, each of them senior Democrats, emerged as leading supporters of elementary and secondary credits: Daniel D. Rostenkowski of Illinois, James A. Burke of Massachusetts, and Charles A. Vanik of Ohio, also the bill's sponsor.[14]

The efforts of interest groups representing private schools

13. "College Tuition," *1976 Congressional Quarterly Almanac* (Washington, D.C.: Congressional Quarterly, 1976), p. 21, 66-S.

14. "Tuition Tax Credit Fails Under Veto Threat," *1978 Congressional Quarterly Almanac* (Washington, D.C.: Congressional Quarterly, 1978), p. 249.

were more than matched by opposition from others claiming to represent the interests of public schools. The newly formed National Coalition to Save Public Education gathered 500 lobbyists in Washington, and the nation's largest teachers union, the National Education Association, had 170 members on Capital Hill with "their energies focused in one place."[15] The National Congress of Parents and Teachers brought in operatives from each of the states represented by a member of the Ways and Means Committee. This pressure initially proved effective, as a 20–16 majority on the committee voted to remove the elementary and secondary tax credits from the bill.

Nonetheless, the Democratic leadership on the House Rules Committee agreed to allow the entire House to vote on the issue, in part because influential opponents of tuition tax credits for higher education believed the bill would be less likely to be enacted if the elementary and secondary credits were included. Their expectations were realized, though not immediately. After narrowly adopting a new amendment from Vanik to reinsert the credits for elementary and secondary education, the House on June 1 passed the bill by a 237–158 vote.

Opposition lobbyists attributed their failure in the House to their relatively late engagement with the issue; many members had declared their support for elementary and secondary credits before the opposition coalesced. Regardless, they were buoyed by the fact that support for the bill remained substantially shy of the two-thirds majority that would be necessary, should President Carter follow through on his threat to veto. Whether or not Carter would face that decision depended on events in the Senate.

15. The quote is from NEA president John Ryor in the *1978 Congressional Quarterly Almanac*, p. 249.

1978: Defeat in the Senate

On August 3 the Senate Finance Committee reported its own tuition tax credit bill. William V. Roth (R-Del.), Robert W. Packwood (R-Ore.), and Daniel Patrick Moynihan (D-N.Y.) co-sponsored the proposal, which closely matched the House-passed bill in its basic structure. While Roth had long advocated tuition tax credits for higher education, Packwood and Moynihan were strong proponents of elementary and secondary credits.

Earlier that year, Packwood and Moynihan had put forward another, more generous tuition tax credit proposal. Their initial proposal offered credits with a maximum value of $500 per child, as opposed to $250 in the House-passed bill, and were fully refundable for families without tax liabilities. The refundability provision, which would have necessitated a $117 million appropriation in fiscal year 1979, led the bill to be referred to multiple committees. In Appropriations, Ernest F. Hollings (D-S.C.) vigorously opposed the bill. After an initial attempt to prevent the bill from even reaching the floor, he moved to report it with a negative recommendation. The following day the Budget Committee, too, reported its requisite waiver resolution unfavorably, leaving the bill little chance of success. Suitably chastened, Packwood and Moynihan withdrew their prefered proposal and adopted an approach more in line with the provisions of the House-passed bill.

As in the House, the status of elementary and secondary school tuition expenses dominated the Senate's discussion of the broader tuition tax credit legislation. Some of the most vocal critics of the elementary and secondary credits worried about their implications for segregation and the quality of education available to black students. Kaneaster Hodges (D-Ark.), for example, complained that the bill would "cause resegregation, and give aid and comfort to those who are trying to avoid integrated schools in the South."[16] To forestall such concerns, Packwood and Moynihan had included provisions excluding tuition at schools found to be discriminatory and mandating the creation of a cabinet-level committee to study the credits' impact on segregation. A last-minute Moynihan amendment went further, explicitly designating the maintenance of diversity a fundamental educational goal. The amendment was adopted with unanimous support.

Other opponents of the bill questioned whether the credits were constitutional. Packwood and Moynihan readily admitted that the issue was not clear-cut, but argued that the only way to settle the matter was to pass the bill and let the courts decide. Moynihan ultimately offered another amendment that wrote this uncertainty into the bill itself in an attempt to placate those who felt Congress was overstepping its bounds. The amendment deleted from the preamble of the bill a clause declaring the credits to be constitutional, substituting in its place language indicating that this was an issue for the courts to decide. The Senate adopted this final amendment with a 56–42 vote.

Yet despite these efforts, Moynihan was ultimately unable to navigate the bill safely through the full Senate. The public school lobby again coordinated opposition, arguing that the measure would undermine support for public education, leading to massive funding cuts. When Senator Hollings offered an amendment deleting the elementary and secondary credits, the Senate adopted the measure by a 56–41 vote.

16. Ibid., p. 254.

The House-Senate Conference: No Common Ground

On September 28, the House-Senate conference committee formed to iron out differences between the two chambers' bills approved a compromise version without the controversial elementary and secondary credits. House conferees Vanik, Rostenkowski, and Burke, apparently uninterested in college tax credits that would not also benefit private and parochial elementary and secondary schools, declined to sign the conference report. While dropping the elementary and secondary credits clearly diminished the enthusiasm of supporters, opposition to the bill remained fierce. The National Coalition to Save Public Education argued that tax credits for higher education would set a harmful precedent that could later be expanded to encompass compulsory schooling.

On October 12, the House voted to recommit the conference report with clear instructions to reinsert the elementary and secondary credits. Their insistence sealed the fate of the entire tax credit bill, which only six months earlier had been expected to sail through Congress without a hitch. The conference committee made one last attempt to design a bill acceptable to both houses, but the Senate rejected the compromise version offering credits for college and secondary (but not elementary) school tuition by voice vote.

Equity and Cost

In addition to issues of race and constitutionality, the 1978 defeat of tuition tax credits also reflected concerns regarding equity and cost. President Carter justified his opposition to higher-education tax credits on the grounds that they would go disproportionately to wealthy families and exclude entirely low-income families who did not pay income taxes. Joseph A.

Califano, Carter's Secretary of Health, Education, and Welfare, told the Ways and Means Committee that the administration was convinced that "many middle income families will invest the same amount of money in higher education regardless of the credit," making the tax credit nothing more than a "general form of tax relief."[17] As an alternative, the administration proposed an increase in the size of Basic Educational Opportunity Grants (BEOG) for higher education available to low-income students.

Several members of Congress attempted to address Carter's concerns within the tax credit framework. Howard M. Metzenbaum (D-Ohio), for example, offered an amendment to the Senate bill that would have phased out the credits for families with annual incomes above $30,000, with families earning more than $40,000 completely ineligible. However, Metzenbaum's amendment failed after opponents argued that the increasing cost of higher education affected families with incomes well above $40,000. Rep. Michael J. Harrington (D-Mass.), who had recently retired from public office on the grounds that he could not afford to send his children to college on his $57,500 congressional salary, poignantly illustrated their claim.[18]

Limiting eligibility for tuition tax credits would also have reduced the program's total cost. Supporters of the Metzenbaum amendment claimed that it would reduce expenses by more than $2 billion. But many budget hawks worried less about the credits' immediate fiscal impact than about their long-term consequences. Budget Committee Chairman Edmund S. Muskie (D-Maine) called the tuition tax credit bill

17. Testimony of Secretary of Health, Education, and Welfare Joseph A. Califano, Jr., before the U.S. Congress, House of Representatives, Committee on Ways and Means, *Hearings on Tax Credits for Nonpublic Education*, 92d Congress, 2d sess., August 1972.

18. *1978 Congressional Quarterly Almanac*, pp. 254–55.

a "Trojan Horse," that "would unleash our worst domestic enemies—more deficit spending, more inflation and more unbal-
anced budgets."[19] Equally colorful language was heard in the
House, where George E. Danielson (D-Calif.) warned his colleagues that the idea of tuition tax credits "is only the nose of
the camel under the flap of the tent, and once this idea gets in,
it will grow and grow."[20]

To avoid such concerns regarding universal tuition tax
credits, Senator Moynihan in 1980 opened a new front in the
battle for government aid for nonpublic schools. Moynihan
proposed to make BEOG grants available to students in private
elementary and secondary schools, with eligible families
receiving a grant of up to $750 a year for each child in private
school. "Baby BEOGs," as he called them, would be restricted
to parents earning less than $20,000 annually. Moreover,
unlike most previous tax credit proposals, the grants would
have benefited even families without tax liabilities. The new
strategy, similar in structure to subsequent voucher schemes,
failed to win new converts and was defeated by a large majority.

1981: New Faces, Same Result

In retrospect, the decision of Moynihan—long the most out-
spoken proponent of tuition tax credits for elementary and secondary education in either body of Congress—to propose an
alternative foreshadows their later withdrawal from the policy
agenda. Yet tuition tax credits continued to generate legislative
interest well into the 1980s. In fact, the combination of Ronald
Reagan's election as president and the Republican takeover of
the Senate in 1980 led to considerable optimism among tax

19. Quoted in ibid., p. 254.
20. Ibid., p. 252.

credit proponents. The Senate's new composition led Moynihan to declare his "impression . . . that we now have a majority for the bill."[21] Sheldon E. Steinbach, general counsel for the American Council on Education and a member of the President-elect's task force on education policy, was more emphatic, calling the election results "a mandate for tuition tax credits."[22] In early 1981 Moynihan and Packwood attempted to capitalize on the opportunity by co-sponsoring another bill offering families a tax credit of up to $250 for each student enrolled in a private school.

Yet the strengthened position of credit advocates only served to increase the sense of urgency among their opponents. On June 8, a coalition of 400 organizations delivered 100,000 letters to the offices of Moynihan and the junior senator from New York, Republican Alfonse D'Amato. American Federation of Teachers (AFT) president Albert Shanker left reporters at the scene with no doubts as to what he believed to be at stake: "This is not a teacher issue," he asserted. "The issue is the future of public education."[23] Though rabbis, Roman Catholic bishops, and leaders of the Moral Majority all testified before the Finance Committee in favor of the bill, no action was taken once the bill reached the Senate floor.

1982–1983: Reagan and Tax Credits

In 1982 the Reagan administration assumed a more active role in support of tuition tax credits. Reagan announced his administration's proposal in a speech delivered on April 15 to a

21. Quoted in Marjorie Hunter, "Proponents of Tuition Tax Credits Optimistic as a Result of Election," *New York Times*, Novermber 17, 1980, p. D11.

22. Quoted in Dan Morgan, "GOP Victory Greatly Aids Chances of Enacting Tuition Tax Credits," *Washington Post*, November 8, 1980, p. A5.

23. Quoted in "2 Senators Given 100,000 Letters Opposing Tuition Tax-Credit Plan," *New York Times*, June 9, 1981, p. B14.

Chicago gathering of the National Catholic Educational Association: "I believe that Americans are over-taxed and under-appreciated and I have come to Chicago to offer relief."[24] Reagan's comments suggest his administration viewed tuition tax credits as a useful weapon in their ongoing struggle with Democrats for the allegiances of Catholic and blue-collar voters. The Democrats, their hands tied by their increasingly close relationship with the teachers unions, were unable to respond.

Reagan's plan, which he submitted to Congress on June 23, called for tax credits equal to 50 percent of tuition up to a maximum of $100 in 1983, $300 in 1984, and $500 in subsequent years. Families with gross incomes of more than $75,000 would be ineligible for the credit, which would begin to be phased out for families with incomes above $50,000. The Senate Finance Committee reported a modified version of this proposal to the Senate floor on September 23.

In spite of its measured approach, the proposal's cost still left Reagan with a formidable political challenge. With budget deficits growing in the wake of his 1981 tax cut, the president had already called for a reduction in federal spending on education. A simultaneous increase in funding for private education could only be interpreted as a slap in the face of the nation's public schools. As National Education Association (NEA) president Willard McGuire put it, "There can be no justification for spending billions of dollars for private and church-related schools at a time when the Reagan administration says it can't afford to support the public schools."[25] With

24. Quoted in Herbert H. Denton, "Tuition Tax Credit Plan Is Outlined; Reagan Urges Cut as 'Equity' for Working Families," *Washington Post*, April 16, 1982, p. A1.
25. Quoted in "Tuition Tax Credit" *1982 Congressional Quarterly Almanac* (Washington, D.C.: Congressional Quarterly, 1978), p. 489.

Hollings threatening to organize a filibuster, no action was taken on the bill.

The fact that fiscal concerns remained an obstacle to the enactment of tuition tax credits even when they were broken off from aid for college students is initially puzzling. As economists pointed out at the time, by inducing additional families to move from the public to private schools, tuition tax credits can actually *reduce* total government spending on education.[26] But any benefits associated with reductions in expenditures as a result of pupil migration would have accrued primarily to the states and localities, which were responsible for the bulk of spending on public education. The short-run implications for the federal budget were undeniably negative.

Two outside events caused the 1983 debate over tuition tax credits to differ from previous renditions. The first was the April release of *A Nation at Risk*, the heavily publicized report of Secretary of Education T. H. Bell's National Commission on Excellence in Education.[27] *A Nation at Risk* mentioned neither tuition tax credits nor any other form of choice-based reform. Yet by drawing attention to the deteriorating performance of American high schools, the report increased interest in the policy's implications—both good and bad—for the quality of

26. E. G. West, "The real costs of tuition tax credits." *Public Choice* 46 (1985): 61–70. West estimated that in the case of the $300 tax credit the Reagan administration proposed in 1983 only 1 percent of public school students would have to transfer to private schools in order for the government to "break even." This estimate rested on a number of dubious assumptions. Specifically, West assumed that the elasticity of supply for private education was infinite, that the marginal costs of public education were equal to average costs per student, and that the public schools would not be able to use their political influence to maintain current expenditure levels despite falling enrollments. Still, the proposals "real" costs would clearly have been less than contemporary estimates indicated.

27. National Commission on Excellence in Education, *A Nation at Risk* (Washington, D.C.: Government Printing Office, 1983).

public education. Advocates spoke more frequently about the
salubrious effects of competition, while the NEA and the AFT
warned that tuition tax credits would jeopardize the nascent
excellence movement by diverting resources from the public
schools.

The second external shock was the Supreme Court's June
29 decision in *Mueller v. Allen* upholding a relatively small
Minnesota state income tax deduction for tuition, textbooks,
and transportation expenses available to both public and private school students.[28] Senator Moynihan cautiously wel-
comed the *Mueller* decision as a "message to Congress that
such tax relief measures to help parents educate their children
are not *de facto* unconstitutional," and even Albert Shanker
admitted that "the Supreme Court decision will provide some
new life to tax credit supporters," enabling them to "pick up a
few votes" in Congress.[29]

Yet speculation in the press that tuition tax credits might
"go further this time" proved mistaken as fiscal considerations
were again decisive.[30] The Reagan administration's proposal
offered tax credits rather than tax deductions and did not
include public school students, leaving the relevance of the
Mueller decision unclear. Extending the credits to include
public school students would have substantially increased
their expected cost, making it politically infeasible. Ultimately, an amendment from Senator Robert Dole (R-Kan.) to
attach tuition tax credits to a minor tariff bill was defeated 59–

28. 463 U.S. 756 (1973).

29. Quoted in Felicity Barringer, "Tuition Tax Credit Advocates Sing
Muted Hosannas," *Washington Post*, June 30, 1983, p. A13; see also Robert
Pear, "Ruling Touches Off New Debate on Prospects of Tuition Tax Credits,"
New York Times, June 30, 1983, p. D23.

30. Curtis J. Sitomer, "Why the Tuition Tax Credit Push May Go Further
This Time," *Christian Science Monitor*, May 11, 1983, p. 3.

38, a margin of defeat wide enough to generate widespread doubts about their future political viability.[31]

From Tax Credits to Vouchers

The close of the 1983 legislative session would prove to be the last time for nearly two decades that Congress would devote sustained attention to tuition tax credits for elementary and secondary education. The disappearance of tuition tax credits from the legislative agenda is closely associated with the emergence of school vouchers as a credible policy proposal. Secretary of Education William J. Bennett entered office in 1985 as a vocal supporter of both policies.[32] But tuition tax credits were notably absent from the administration's 1986 budget proposal. The administration instead put forward a plan to convert Title I, the existing federal compensatory education program for disadvantaged students in public schools, into a program that would give low-income families the option of a $600 voucher to help send their children to private schools.

Although ultimately unsuccessful, the idea of converting Title I money into portable vouchers had much to recommend it politically, especially in view of the administration's disappointing experience with tuition tax credits. First, Title I vouchers would be restricted to students from low-income families, making it impossible for the program to be criticized as welfare for the rich. Furthermore, since the Title I proposal essentially amounted to a change in how an existing program

31. A similar proposal introduced in the House Ways and Means Committee by Bill Gradison (R-Ohio) failed even to make it out of committee. Among the leading opponents of Gradison's bill was Democratic committee chairman Dan Rostenkowski, who since 1978 had adopted his party's stated position on the issue.

32. William J. Bennett, *The De-valuing of America* (New York: Summit Books, 1992).

was administered, it would not require an increase in federal spending on education (although it would surely have attracted attention in the courts if it included religious schools).

The withdrawal of Republican support for tuition tax credits continued under Reagan's successor. George H. W. Bush initially distanced himself from the issue, choosing not to discuss it during the 1988 campaign.[33] Then, in a May 1989 appearance with a group of seventy-five high school students invited to the White House, a private school student from Hawaii asked the President if his parents should receive a tax break. "No they shouldn't," Bush replied, and proceeded to elaborate on his position. "I think everyone should support the public school system and then if on top of that your parents think they want to shell out, in addition to the tax money, tuition money, that's their right."[34]

Tuition Tax Credits and the
Politics of Tax Expenditures

A variety of factors make it a commonplace among political scientists that tax expenditures are more easily passed than

33. Barbara Vobejda, "New ABCs for Campaigning on Education; Bush Quiet on School Prayer, Tuition Tax Credits; Dukakis Urges Modest Programs," *Washington Post*, September 18, 1988, p. A11.

34. Quoted in "Bush Comes Out Against Private-Tuition Tax Credits," *St. Louis Post-Dispatch*, May 30, 1989, p. 4B. While rejecting tuition tax credits, Bush continued to press Congress to accept school vouchers. His budget proposal for 1992 included a $500 million voucher plan, the "GI Bill for Kids," that would have provided $1,000 vouchers for low- and middle-income families. Lynn Olson and Julie A. Miller, "Self-Styled 'Education President' President Places His Case Before Voters," *Education Week* (February 12, 1992).

direct government spending programs.[35] During much of the twentieth century legislators simply "had better information about the costs of direct expenditures than about the costs of tax expenditures." Moreover, while the creation of a direct spending program typically requires new legislation, "tax expenditures can be tucked away in must-pass revenue bills." Tax expenditures also often lend themselves to "strategic representation"—that is, they can be defended on a variety of different grounds, broadening their appeal. Because tax expenditures are authorized and funded by the same committee in Congress, "[t]he number of possible veto points in Congress is . . . cut in half."[36] Finally, it is notable that the committees with jurisdiction over tax policymaking, the House Ways and Means Committee and the Senate Finance Committee, are among the most influential in their respective chambers.

In the case of tuition tax credit proposals in the 1970s and 1980s, however, these advantages proved insufficient to deliver legislative success, calling into question the usefulness of the tax expenditure framework as the primary lens through which to view this issue. Tuition tax credits did not reach the legislative agenda until after the 1969 publication of the first official budget for tax expenditures had revealed the scope of this previously "hidden" component of American social pol-

35. Christopher Howard, *The Hidden Welfare State: Tax Expenditures and Social Policy in the United States* (Princeton, N.J.: Princeton University Press, 1997), p. 178. Howard's thorough study is only the latest piece of research to reach this conclusion, and also the most relevant given its focus on tax expenditures as an instrument of social policy. Earlier works include Theodore J. Eismeier, "The Power Not to Tax: A Search for Effective Controls," *Journal of Policy Analysis and Management* 1, no. 3 (1982): 333–45; John F. Witte, *The Politics and Development of the Federal Income Tax* (Madison: University of Wisconsin Press, 1985).

36. Howard, *Hidden Welfare State*, pp. 178–80.

icy. Meanwhile, the Budget and Impoundment Control Act of 1974 ensured that most subsequent House revenue bills would be considered under rules allowing amendments deleting and modifying specific provisions on the House floor. By reducing the revenue committees' dominance, these two changes opened tax policymaking to greater involvement on the part of interest groups.

Unlike most tax expenditures, the way the cost of tuition tax credits was calculated actually made them an especially easy target for criticism. By ignoring the potential implications of pupil migration from the public to the private sector, the official reports produced by Congress and later by the Reagan administration typically *over*estimated their costs, at least for the government as a whole. Moreover, the policy's immediate costs were not alone in attracting close scrutiny. Oft-expressed fears that tuition tax credits, if enacted, would grow more expensive over time suggest that many members of Congress had been burned in the past by tax expenditures and were disinclined to let that happen again. The salience of these concerns is evident from the fact that the tuition tax credit bills passed by each chamber in 1978 were slated to expire within three years, a rarity for tax expenditures.[37]

At various points, proponents of tuition tax credits did attempt to facilitate their passage by attaching them to other legislative vehicles. A case in point is Senator Buckley's unsuccessful effort to add them to the 1976 Tax Reform Bill. Similar strategic considerations explain the decision of Senators Packwood and Moynihan in 1978 to fold their proposal into Senator Roth's tax credit bill for higher education, a bill expected to generate widespread popular support. But as the latter example demonstrates, tuition tax credits for elementary

37. Howard, *Hidden Welfare State*, p. 90.

and secondary education were controversial enough to bring down otherwise popular pieces of legislation.

This controversy often reflected genuine substantive concerns regarding their implications for segregation and public school quality, as well as doubts about their constitutionality. But these anxieties were transformed into effective political influence largely by the highly coordinated efforts of a diverse coalition of interest groups under the leadership of the teachers unions. The unions' opposition to tuition tax credits is entirely understandable. By threatening to increase the number of students attending private schools (or at least to stave off its decline), tuition tax credits were in conflict with the unions' basic goal of expanding their ranks and limiting competition. Moreover, the sheer volume of economic and electoral resources at their disposal made politicians receptive to their concerns.[38] Significantly, the only bill containing tuition tax credits for elementary and secondary education to survive a floor vote in Congress came up at a time when the opposition admitted it had been caught off guard and was late in beginning its lobbying efforts.

The interests and influence of the public school lobby also help account for the failure of strategic representation to placate opposition to tuition tax credits sufficiently for them to gain passage. Advocates of tuition tax credits certainly defended them on multiple grounds, often simultaneously. The credits were presented as aid to private and parochial schools, tax relief for the families who attended them, and— especially following the 1983 release of *A Nation at Risk*—a

---

38. On the interests of teachers unions, see Terry M. Moe, "The Future of School Vouchers," this volume; on their political resources, including their capacity to turn out voters, see Moe's "Political Control and the Power of the Agent," Annual Meeting of the Midwest Political Science Association, April 2003, Chicago.

way to generate quality improvement in the public sector. Yet none of these justifications could change the mind of the suppliers of public education, who remained "unalterably opposed" to legislation providing tax credits for private school tuition expenses.[39]

Finally, most of the tuition tax credit proposals taken up in Congress during this period offered credits to all families with students in private schools. Owing to budget constraints, these credits were necessarily small in size. This approach made it difficult for politicians to mobilize intense support for the programs among any one segment of the population. It also subjected the policies to criticism on the grounds that too large a portion of the benefits would go to the relatively wealthy, and that they were too small to allow the relatively poor to gain access to the private sector.

Moreover, by benefiting only those families with positive tax liabilities, most tuition tax credit proposals excluded altogether the most disadvantaged segment of the population, including many of those with the greatest interest in moving their child to a private school. Making the credits refundable would have allowed them to reach much of this group. However, as Senators Packwood and Moynihan learned in 1978, adopting this tactic meant forgoing the advantage of approval and funding from a single Congressional committee. Proponents of tuition tax credits therefore faced a catch-22: designing tuition tax credits that were both equitable and large enough to make a substantive difference to parents' educational choices decreased the likelihood of legislative success.

In short, by the mid-1970s tax expenditures had become such an important and expensive part of American social pol-

---

39. National Education Association, *Tuition Tax Credits* (NEA Government Relations, 1982).

icy that their costs were no longer ignored. Indeed, they may even have been subjected to additional scrutiny. The fact that the tuition tax credits under consideration were to be offered by a level of government with little financial responsibility for public education meant that the expected costs were not insubstantial. Equally important was the existence of an established universal system of government-provided services in competition with the private providers who would benefit from the tax break, a challenge that has not confronted most other tax expenditures. Regardless of how politicians presented tuition tax credits and the legislative vehicle they chose, the public school lobby remained opposed, quite simply because it was in their interests to do so. This structural opposition, deeply rooted in the electoral incentives and partisan ties of legislators, repeatedly gave the lie to brief moments of optimism among the policy's supporters following favorable election results or encouraging news from the courts.

State Tuition Tax Credits: The Political Future

Yet tuition tax credits have reappeared on the agenda, with new programs already established in several states and discussions under way in others and in Congress. The state-level programs now in place in Minnesota, Illinois, and Iowa resemble earlier federal proposals—that is, they reduce the tax liabilities of all eligible families with children in private schools. The greater degree of success tax credit legislation has achieved at the state level is consistent with the observation that the states are better positioned than the federal government to reap any fiscal gains from students switching to the private sector.[40]

40. The extent to which states and districts would gain fiscally from a reduction in the number of pupils enrolled in public schools is a matter of

Three other states have been more innovative, designing tax credit programs in such a way as to increase their effectiveness and political support. In 1998 Arizona introduced a nonrefundable state income tax credit of up to $625 for contributions to Student Tuition Organizations that disburse scholarships to families with children in private schools. Although there are no statutory restrictions on eligibility for the scholarships, the majority of participating organizations claim to distribute their scholarships according to need.[41]

By providing awards concurrent with actual enrollment in a private school, the scholarship approach has a significant advantage in targeting low-income students even over refundable tax credits, which typically require families to wait up to a year after making a tuition payment to receive their subsidy. Moreover, the use of scholarship organizations may give the program an edge over voucher systems that do not provide families with assistance in choosing a private school or securing a place for their child: scholarship organizations may come to see the placement of students as part of their mission.[42]

The scholarship organization approach also expands the number of potential participants in the program, since even families without children are eligible to claim the credit. This alone may lead to enhanced popular support, assuming that people value the opportunity to donate money to a scholarship

---

considerable debate. It is unlikely that spending would decrease by the full value of average per-pupil expenditures, at least in the short run. But the long-run productivity gains from increased competition could be substantial, leading to even larger spending reductions.

41. Carrie Lips and Jennifer Jacoby, "The Arizona Scholarship Tax Credit: Giving Parents Choices, Saving Taxpayers Money," *Cato Institute Policy Analysis*, no. 414, p. 1.

42. The fact that the Arizona legislation requires credit-eligible organizations to distribute at least 90 percent of their revenues each year as scholarships may hinder their ability to pursue this goal effectively.

organization. That they do seems apparent from the growing number of taxpayers participating in the program. In 1998, the first year of the program, 4,247 taxpayers made contributions to fifteen different scholarship organizations; by 2000, 37,368 taxpayers made contributions to thirty-four organizations.[43]

Similar programs established by Pennsylvania and Florida in 2001 offer corporations rather than individual taxpayers tax credits for donations to scholarship organizations.[44] Pennsylvania allocates its credits on a first-come, first-served basis, up to a maximum of $20 million each year for the entire state. Despite the fact that the program does not allow businesses to recover the full value of their donation, the upper limit was easily reached during the program's first year. Apparently Pennsylvania businesses place a substantial positive value on the ability to contribute money to local scholarship organizations rather than send it to Harrisburg, perhaps because of the positive media coverage generated. The establishment of a reasonable upper limit on donations goes a long way toward eliminating uncertainty regarding the amount of scholarship funds that will be available each year. Both Pennsylvania and Florida also set strict limits on eligibility for the funds distributed by participating scholarship organizations, making it difficult to charge that scholarship recipients are not in need of assistance.[45]

43. Lips and Jacoby, "Arizona Scholarship Tax Credit," p. 4.

44. In Florida, businesses can receive a dollar-for-dollar tax credit for donations to scholarship organizations up to 75 percent of their corporate income taxes, with an aggregate limit of $50 million for the state as a whole. In Pennsylvania, businesses receive a tax credit equal to 75 percent of the value of their donation, with a maximum credit for a single company $100,000 annually. The value of the credit grows to 90 percent if they are willing to make a two-year commitment.

45. Eligibility for scholarships in Pennsylvania is limited to families with a household income level of $50,000 or less, with an additional allowance of $10,000 for each eligible student and dependent member of the household.

A final design innovation has been the strategic packaging of tuition tax credits with similar programs benefiting public schools and their employees. Arizona legislators paired tax credits for donations to scholarship organizations with smaller credits of up to $200 for cash contributions to local public schools or fees paid for extracurricular activities. Scholars have since criticized these credits on equity grounds, since the schools with the least disadvantaged students receive the lion's share of the donations.[46] Nevertheless, they played a key role in securing the program's passage. Pennsylvania's tax credit program similarly provides $10 million in credits for donations to public school foundations funding "innovative educational programs." The enthusiastic response of scattered superintendents to the windfalls generated for their districts has helped to offset criticism of the program from the state teachers union.[47]

Although the distribution of responsibility for funding education of education finance suggests that the outlook for school choice programs is most promising at the state level, constitutional issues suggest caution. As if to illustrate this point, only weeks following the *Zelman* decision a Florida Circuit Court judge struck down his state's voucher program, citing the state constitution's "clear and unambiguous" prohibition on the use of public money to attend sectarian schools.[48] The

---

Florida limits eligibility to students eligible for the national free or reduced-price school lunch under the National School Lunch Act.

46. Glen Y. Wilson, "The Equity Impact of Arizona's Education Tax Credit Program: A Review of the First Three Years (1998–2000)," Education Policy Studies Library, Arizona State University.

47. Jan Murphy, "Public Schools Give Tax Program an 'A'," *The Patriot-News*, June 17, 2002.

48. *Holmes v. Bush*, No. CV 99-370, slip op. (Fla. Cir. Ct. August 5, 2002.). Quoted in Michael A. Fletcher, "Florida's Voucher Law Is Struck Down;

constitutions of forty-seven states contain establishment provisions that are more restrictive than the federal establishment
clause.[49] Although some of these provisions have been interpreted narrowly, the Florida decision confirms that others
remain a substantial obstacle to future voucher programs.

Tuition tax credits largely avoid this difficulty. Consider
the argument of the Arizona Supreme Court in *Kotterman v.
Killian*, its 1999 ruling upholding the Arizona Tax Credit for
Education Program:

> No money *ever* enters the state's control as a result of this tax
> credit. Nothing is deposited in the state treasury or other
> accounts under the management or possession of govern-
> mental agencies or public officials. Thus, under any common
> understanding of the words, we are not here dealing with
> "public money."[50]

As the majority goes on to explain, a court ruling that a tax
credit constitutes public money would effectively be forced to
argue that all money is the government's, and that individuals
are allowed to keep a certain portion of it for their own private
use.[51] The constitutional status of tuition tax credits is therefore quite favorable and seems likely to remain so, if only
because of the difficulty of coming up with a defensible legal
standard that would define them as public money.

This legal difference has important political implications.
Private schools may be less fearful of the threat of government
regulation following the establishment of tuition tax credits
than they are for vouchers, and therefore more likely to mobilize to support the policy. And surely state legislators are more

---

Court Says States Constitution Bars Public Support of Parochial Schools,"
Washington Post, August 6, 2002.
  49. Clint A. Bolick, "Sunshine Replaces the Cloud," this volume.
  50. 193 Ariz. 273, 972 P.2d 606 (1999), p. 21.
  51. Ibid., p. 23.

likely to give their support to a school choice program they do not expect to face a legal challenge. School choice proponents have already filed test cases in multiple states in the hopes of a Supreme Court ruling that state constitutional provisions forbidding the use of public funds in religious schools are unconstitutional under the free exercise clause.[52] Until such a ruling, however, tuition tax credits will continue to have a considerable advantage over vouchers in a number of states.

Conclusion

Small in size, broad in scope, and originating from a level of government with minimal fiscal responsibility for public education, the tuition tax credit programs proposed and debated in Congress in the 1970s and 1980s had crucial flaws that recent state-level programs have managed to address. With a state income tax in place in all but seven states and a corporate income tax in all but three, the administrative structure for similar programs to be enacted in a large number of states is already in place. Moreover, the budget difficulties currently facing the states should make the possibility of reducing public expenditure on education especially attractive.

The most likely course of events therefore may be a gradual proliferation of state-level tuition tax credit programs, varied in their features as states continue to experiment with alternative policy designs. The process will undoubtedly be measured, as experiments with vouchers continue and opponents of school choice continue to exert considerable political influence. Yet it is also likely to be steady, as new tuition tax credit programs build support among beneficiaries, making them difficult to repeal.

52. Bolick, "Sunshine Replaces the Cloud."

8   The Future of Charter Schools

BRYAN HASSEL

With the Supreme Court's endorsement of public voucher programs involving religious schools in the *Zelman* case, the nation suddenly faces the possibility of a significant expansion of programs that provide publicly funded scholarships for students to attend private schools. Substantial barriers still exist to such expansion, primarily in state constitutions and in the political arena, but it seems likely that in at least some cities and states, advocates will succeed in creating new voucher programs with the potential to serve large numbers of children.

The prospect of larger-scale private school choice programs raises the question of *supply*: what schools will be available to voucher-bearing families? Preexisting private schools are the most obvious candidates; but there are various limits on the capacity of the existing private sector to serve children in a voucher program. Some private schools may not want to participate in a school choice program because of strings that may be attached to public funding. Constraints on tuition, requirements to admit students by lottery, or accountability and reporting mandates will make some private schools think participation is not worth the price. Other private schools may simply not want to expand their enrollment beyond their current levels. They may be the size they are by choice and regard it as part of their distinctive nature; becoming larger could undermine their school cultures or their appeal to their current "customers." One set of private schools that would be eager to offer slots to voucher-bearing students is schools that have trouble enrolling enough students to make ends meet; although such schools could provide some capacity to a choice program, they may not be the most attractive sources of supply. Presumably, most families will want their children to attend successful private schools, not struggling ones.

So while existing private schools may meet some of the demand for an expanded voucher initiative, it is likely that a significant source of supply would need to come from *newly formed schools*. What are the prospects for this kind of new-school creation in the context of a voucher program? In Milwaukee, some 107 schools enrolled more than 10,000 voucher-bearing students during the 2001–2002 school year.[1] Of these, 67 were in existence prior to 1990, the year the program began.[2] The other 40 formed since 1990. Since the overall private school population in Milwaukee declined during the 1990s, it seems plausible that these 40 schools, which together educate 37 percent of the choice program's students, were formed largely in response to the availability of vouchers.[3] If one envi-

1. Public Policy Forum, "Choice Schools Enroll Fewer K–4 Students," *Public Policy Forum Research Brief* 90, no. 1 (January 2002).

2. Author's tabulations from unpublished data provided by Emily Van Dunk and Anneliese Dickman, Public School Forum, 2002. Three of these schools were actually founded after 1989, but they were formed as a result of mergers of preexisting schools and thus were not truly new starts.

3. Public Policy Forum, "Despite Expansion of Choice Program, Number of City Children in Private School Has Not Increased," *Public Policy Forum In Fact* 87, no. 13 (December 1999).

sions a nationwide voucher-bearing population of one million children (100 times the size of Milwaukee), and if one extrapolates the Milwaukee experience with new starts, 4,000 new schools would be required to meet the demands of choice.

For this larger-scale perspective it is helpful to look at the charter school movement, which has been the country's most substantial venue for new-school creation over the last decade. Some 2,700 charter schools educated nearly 685,000 students nationwide in 2002–2003.[4] Charter schools are public schools operated by independent or quasi-independent organizations under a "charter," or contract, with an entity empowered by state law to authorize charter schools. Like private schools under voucher programs, they are schools of choice and have the freedom to implement their chosen educational approaches. But they typically face more constraints than private schools when it comes to compliance with state and federal mandates, their uses of funds, and accountability and reporting. In the 1998–99 school year, the most recent year for which complete data are available, 72 percent of charter schools were newly formed schools. Eighteen percent had previously been district public schools, with the remaining 10 percent converted private schools.[5] If those proportions still apply to the charter school population in 2002–2003, approximately 1,940 of the 2,700 charter schools in that school year were newly formed schools.[6] This is only about half of what would be required to service a million-child voucher experiment, but at least it begins to approach that sort of magnitude.

4. See Bryan C. Hassel, "Friendly Competition," *Education Next* 3, no. 1 (Winter 2003): 8–15.

5. RPP International, *The State of Charter Schools: Fourth-Year Report* (Washington, D.C.: U.S. Department of Education, 2000), p. 14.

6. Center for Education Reform, *Back-to-School Bulletin* 4, no. 38 (September 17, 2002).

After rapid initial growth in new starts, the expansion of the charter school movement has leveled off. This leveling is partly due to constraints in public policy—as legislatures have imposed caps or other restrictions that make it difficult for more charter schools to form in some states. But the charter school movement also seems to be plateauing because of challenges of *supply*—an apparent dearth of individuals and organizations with the willingness and capacity to start new schools.

This chapter discusses those supply challenges, what might be done about them, and what they mean for the prospects of expanded voucher programs. The next section explains the supply challenges in more detail. The following sections explore alternative paths to solving the new-school supply problem. The concluding section considers the implications of the discussion for voucher programs.

The Charter School Supply Challenge

Nationally, the growth of charter schools was dramatic in the first years following the passage of the initial charter laws (see Table 1). In 2001 and 2002, though, the number of new charter schools opening in the fall actually declined compared to the previous years. And the percentage growth in charter schools has tapered off from the heady three-digit rates of the mid-1990s.

Statutory caps on charter schools have caused some of this leveling, but not all of it. Even in jurisdictions with few restrictions on new starts, the number of schools opening tends to decline over time. The District of Columbia provides a good example. The D.C. charter law is one of the nation's most open to chartering. The law creates a new entity, the D.C. Public Charter Schools Board, to authorize schools. It does not cap

Table 1. Growth in the Number of Charter Schools Nationally, 1992–1999 through 2002–2003

Year	New Schools	Total Schools	Growth Rate (in percent)
1992–93	2	2	N/A [a]
1993–94	34	36	1,700 [a]
1994–95	64	100	178 [a]
1995–96	154	254	154 [a]
1996–97	178	432	70 [a]
1997–98	289	721	67 [a]
1998–99	401	1,122	56 [a]
1999–00	567	1,689	51 [b]
2000–01	380	2,069	22 [b]
2001–02	362	2,431	17 [b]
2002–03	269	2,700	11 [b]

Sources:
   a. RPP International, *The State of Charter Schools: Fourth-Year Report* (Washington, D.C.: U.S. Department of Education, 2000), p. 11.
   b. Bryan C. Hassel, "Friendly Competition," *Education Next* 3, no. 1 (Winter 2003): 10.

the number of schools. And it provides charter schools with ample resources, including facilities funding. Yet from the high point of fifteen new starts in 1998, the number of new charter schools has declined to eleven in the fall of 1999, to six in 2000, to four in 2001, to just one in 2002.[7] It appears that within a given geographical area, there is a limited supply of entrepreneurs willing to undertake starting a charter school, a supply that gradually peters out—not to zero, but to what amounts to a drop in the bucket of public schooling in a city or state.

Research has begun to suggest some of the reasons for this

7. DC Public Charter School Resource Center, "Facts About DC Public Charter Schools." Available: http://www.dcchartercenter.org/docs/DCCharterFacts.pdf (accessed 12/31/02).

leveling phenomenon.[8] Starting a school completely from scratch is, in a word, difficult. It's become a cliché that charter schools, in addition to being educational institutions, have to succeed as small businesses—balancing their budgets, negotiating leases and financing packages and contracts, making payroll. In states where charter schools are independent, they have to function as mini-school districts as well, with all the attendant reporting and regulatory burdens. Individuals and small teams—often teachers, parents, or community activists who have never run schools—are apt to possess some but not all of these skills and backgrounds. And skills are not the whole story. The start-up of a school also takes an extraordinary amount of time, dedication, and intangible qualities of perseverance and resourcefulness. Even individuals with the apparent expertise needed to start a school may lack these characteristics. So one constraint on supply is the availability of leaders with the capacity to pull off this challenging undertaking.

Opening a new school also requires capital. Most charter schools receive federally funded start-up grants of $10,000 to $150,000 for one to three years. Beyond that, they cannot expect any public funds to flow until, in the best of circumstances, the July before they open. Expenses, however, cannot wait. Principals need to be hired a few months before school starts. Ideally, teachers start at least a few weeks before students arrive. Then there are books and bookshelves, desks and

8. Studies of the challenges of school start-up include: RPP International, *The State of Charter Schools*, pp. 42–46; Noelle Griffin and Priscilla Wohlstetter, "Building a Plane While Flying It: Early Lessons from Developing Charter Schools," *Teachers College Record* 103, no. 2 (April 2001): 336–65; and Bryan C. Hassel, *The Charter School Challenge: Avoiding the Pitfalls, Fulfilling the Promise* (Washington, D.C.: Brookings Institution Press, 1999), chap. 5.

desktop computers, and all the other accoutrements of schooling that need to be purchased.

And all this does not include the greatest charter school start-up cost: facilities. Typically, a charter school does not receive any kind of building in which to operate. Its leaders must find one, renovate one, or build one. In most cases, some kind of capital investment is required. But lenders and landlords tend to be reluctant to extend credit or long-term leases to charter schools. Their existence is tenuous, their management teams often inexperienced. Because they typically do not receive any special funds to make loan and lease payments, repayment is always uncertain. Especially in tough urban real estate markets, the facilities challenge alone places a tight constraint on supply of new schools.[9]

Enter the EMOs

For people interested in a charter school movement that achieves scale, there is one obvious solution to these challenges—operation of more charter schools by "education management organizations," often called EMOs. According to calculations made by the Center for Education Reform, nineteen of these companies ran 350 charter schools in 2001–2002, about 15 percent of the nation's charter schools.[10] Since EMO-run schools are typically larger than average for charter schools, EMO schools actually educate an even higher percentage of charter school *students*—perhaps 25 to 30 percent.

Most EMOs today are for-profit companies, but not all. Aspire Public Schools, for example, is a nonprofit seeking to

9. See Bryan C. Hassel, *Paying for the Charter Schoolhouse* (St. Paul: Charter Friends National Network, 1999).

10. Center for Education Reform, *Public-Private Partnerships: A Consumer's Guide* (Washington, D.C., 2002), p. 1.

operate a large chain of public schools, at least initially in California. The (also nonprofit) New Schools Venture Fund has established a "Charter Accelerator" initiative specifically to invest in more such nonprofit EMOs.

EMOs offer several answers to the supply question:

Expertise and systems. Starting and operating a school requires expertise across a range of fields, from curriculum and instructional design to facilities management to community relations. EMOs can hire experts in these areas or develop expertise over time, and then share knowledge and capacity with their constituent schools. They can turn expertise into systems so that every school doesn't have to reinvent the wheel.

Economies of scale. As they operate more and more schools, EMOs can use their growing buying power to obtain good deals in markets for goods and services. Negotiating bulk purchase contracts with suppliers, they can reduce the per-student cost of equipment, furniture, transportation, food service, accounting, human resources functions, and the like.

Capital (for R&D and possibly facilities). At least in the case of for-profit EMOs, the prospects of long-term profitability and value make it possible for the companies to raise capital from venture investors or, in a smaller number of cases like Edison Schools, the public markets. For nonprofits, philanthropic funds serve a similar purpose. This capital allows the companies to make substantial investments in research and development, such as Edison's multi-year curriculum design project, which took place largely before the company operated a single school. Some EMOs have also deployed capital to help meet the facilities financing challenge.

Incentive and capacity to cultivate leaders. As important as a company's expertise and systems are to its schools, the quality of school-level leadership is still critical for the success of EMO-run schools. Because of the importance of school leadership,

EMOs have strong incentives to seek out high-potential leaders and develop their capabilities over time. And because they operate multiple schools, they are in a position to develop a "farm system" and create opportunities for career advancement that would not be possible in more independent charter schools.

Incentive and capacity to sustain schools over time. If a stand-alone charter school begins to struggle, the founders or current leaders may try strenuously to get the school back on course. But if they fail, there is no institution that is likely to do the hard work of saving the school. The school district may be glad to see the school go; the charter authorizer may not have the capacity or the philosophical inclination to intervene. But if an EMO school begins to sink, the EMO has strong incentives to rescue it. And they may have the resources to do so—sending in new leadership or expertise.

For several reasons, then, it seems probable that if the charter school movement grows, EMOs will continue to grow in importance within it. But it would be a mistake to rely on EMOs alone to sustain the charter school sector over time.

First, though EMOs bring substantial monetary and human resources to the table, they are not immune from financial and management challenges of their own. One of the major national EMOs, National Heritage Academies, recently reported an annual profit. But for most of the scale players in the market, the "for-profit" label has so far been more about aspiration than results. Investments in capacity and marketing have swamped revenues for the typical EMO.

Of course short-term losses are all part of the plan, but financial challenges have still bedeviled EMOs intermittently. In the spring of 2002, for example, Edison Schools faced a severe capital shortage and other financial problems that sent its stock below one dollar a share, down from its peak of $36. The crisis was averted by $40 million in new financing, but investors are still bearish on Edison's prospects, with its share price still measured in cents in early July 2002.

Second, for-profit EMOs create political challenges of their own. Under any circumstances, charter schools ignite political controversy. When schools are operated by for-profit entities, they become even more a lightning rod for criticism. Grassroots organizations like ACORN, which have supported charter schools—and even started their own—have led vigorous campaigns against Edison Schools' involvement in troubled public systems like Philadelphia, New York, and San Francisco.

These experiences raise questions about the political viability of a charter school movement that becomes largely one made up of schools run by for-profit EMOs. Schools arising from the grassroots, run by teachers or parents or neighborhood residents, appear important to maintaining the fragile political coalition that has sustained charter schools so far. Charter school policies have attracted unlikely, perhaps even bizarre coalitions that include free-marketeers and business leaders, but also community-based organizations, civil rights groups, and other nontraditional allies. It seems that the support of nonconservative charter advocates depends, in part, on the fact that up to now the movement mostly consists of grassroots, community-based schools, not franchises of profit-seeking companies.

Nonprofit EMOs present less of a political problem: some community residents may perceive them as "outsiders," but not profiteers. But nonprofit EMO schools are so far only a small fraction of all EMO schools. Of the nineteen companies profiled in a recent Center for Education Reform report, only two were non-profits. Together, they operated just twelve of the 350 EMO schools open in 2001–2002.[11]

Finally, there are reasons to think EMOs may not be the most

11. Ibid.

likely source of breakthrough innovations that could bring the dramatic gains in performance that we need to see in schools. The drive for scale seems to mitigate against out-of-the-box approaches. To begin with, attracting sufficient enrollment is vital for EMOs; the need to fill seats is bound to drive companies to appeal to the "median" consumer, who might balk at grade configurations, pedagogical approaches, or other features that look different from what she is used to seeing.

The companies' own internal dynamics also push toward incrementalism. EMOs face the substantial challenge of scaling up an educational and organizational model across multiple sites, perhaps across a wide geography. It makes sense in that context to select the familiar, the easily conveyed. The same goes for personnel. If a company needs, say, thirty principals, the average hire is more apt to resemble the typical principal than the renegade the board of a one-off charter school might seek. Further, even if an EMO includes some break-the-mold aspects in its initial design, it is unlikely to be an ongoing source of innovation. As business scholars such as Clayton Christensen have found, companies of all kinds tend to make incremental, rather than "disruptive," changes in their products and services over time; the most substantial innovations come from new entrants to markets, not existing players.[12]

To be sure, some EMOs have posted positive results. Edison Schools, for example, reports that from 1995 to 2001, the percentage of its students achieving grade-level standards rose by an average of six points per year.[13] But according to the information presented in the Center for Education Reform's survey of management companies, few have undertaken such comprehensive

12. See Clayton Christensen, *The Innovator's Dilemma* (New York: HarperBusiness, 2000).
13. Edison Schools, *Fourth Annual Report on School Performance* (New York, 2001), p. 4.

analyses.[14] Most can report some positive news in particular years, schools, subjects, or grade levels, but not system-wide success over time.

Different Approaches to the Supply Challenge

If EMOs are not the complete solution to the supply challenge, what is? Addressing this question requires thinking about "scale" in two new ways. First, what would it take to create an environment in which much larger numbers of successful, stand-alone charter schools can form and thrive? Second, what would it take to enable more successful, stand-alone schools to "scale up"—by replicating themselves, or through other means? This section discusses these questions in turn.

What kinds of changes would make it possible for many more stand-alone charter schools to start up and be successful with students? Presently, starting a new school from scratch is too difficult and painful an undertaking even for people who would seem capable of pulling it off. Much of the work goes into activities that have nothing to do with educational innovation and fresh thinking, such as transportation, food service, accounting, regulatory compliance, zoning battles, mortgages. Under these burdens, entrepreneurial energy and enthusiasm can frazzle away. One can guess that there is a large reservoir of entrepreneurial educators and non-educators who would be willing to engage in school start-up—*if* it were not so daunting.

Part of the answer certainly lies in the policy arena—making sure charter schools have equitable access to funding (including capital funds), refraining from burdening schools with needless regulations, ensuring that there are bodies other than local school boards that can issue charters in every juris-

14. *Public-Private Partnerships: A Consumer's Guide.*

diction. As important as these policy issues are, I will focus here on more internal or "supply-side" solutions. Stand-alone charter schools need access to the same high-quality, pooled expertise that the best school systems and EMOs provide to their schools. They need a set of institutions that can shoulder the burdens of school start-up and management, allowing entrepreneurs to focus on building an excellent educational program and organization. But, to retain their independence, stand-alone schools need to come to these service-providers as voluntary, paying customers, not as units controlled by a larger system.

The creative challenge, then, is to imagine a "system" of providers that can deliver this kind of service.[15] What would the attributes of such a system be? Beyond the obvious one— quality—three others seem most important: scope, intensity, and diversity.

Scope. Since operating a school is a complex undertaking, the service infrastructure needs to cover a wide range of issues on which charter school operators may need help—everything from the mechanics of start-up to facilities development to curriculum design to assessment to human resources.

"Help" most often comes in one of two forms: consulting and direct services. With consulting, a provider helps the charter operator make decisions, design systems, analyze problems, and improve the school's own capacity to do its work over time. With direct services, a provider actually steps in to carry out some part of the work of the charter school. Both kinds of help are vital for

---

15. For explorations of this kind of system, see: Chester E. Finn, Jr., Bruno V. Manno, and Gregg Vanourek, *Charter Schools in Action: Renewing Public Education* (Princeton, N.J.: Princeton University Press, 2000), pp. 118–22; Paul T. Hill, Christine Campbell, and James Harvey, *It Takes a City: Getting Serious about Urban School Reform* (Washington, D.C.: Brookings Institution Press, 2000), chap. 4.

stand-alone schools. Direct services shoulder burdens that would otherwise fall on charter entrepreneurs, freeing them to focus on making the school work as well as possible. Consulting helps school leaders make wise choices (including choices about service providers) and improve as the school matures.

It's worth noting that in many of these service areas, an industry of providers already exists—because school districts and private schools already demand the service. Prime examples include textbook and software publishers, information management systems, developers of curricula and "comprehensive school reform models," and transportation providers. In other areas, like accounting, payroll, legal services, and facilities development and financing, a host of general-purpose providers already serve nonprofits and small businesses. Many of these pre-existing companies see great potential in the charter school market and have already begun offering their products and services to charter school customers.

The list also includes a number of services that are not really all that relevant to most school districts. The most obvious of these is start-up assistance. Though operating a school on an ongoing basis has its own difficulties, the tribulations of start-up are perhaps the most threatening to the prospects of stand-alone charter schools. And it clearly does not make sense for every individual charter entrepreneur to master on its own the intricacies of issues as diverse as facilities development, staff recruitment, student marketing, curriculum development, instructional design, the establishment of school record-keeping and accounting systems, and so on. A range of high-quality start-up assistance providers— organizations that can amass expertise in all these areas and help entrepreneurs avoid floundering in basic problems—is a must.

Even where a sector of service-providers already exists, its offerings may not be well tailored to the charter context. Charter schools tend to be small, have limited budgets, and face uncertain futures owing to the vicissitudes of the market and the threat of nonrenewal or revocation. They are often not attractive as customers to conventional providers. Facilities financing stands out as one illustration, but the same holds true for many curriculum and whole school reform providers. While learning programs like Core Knowledge and Expeditionary Learning/Outward Bound have seen real opportunities in the charter sector, others have shied away.

In other words, new institutions will need to arise, both to meet needs that are unique to charter schools and to design service packages in older service areas that make sense for charter schools.

Intensity. One answer to the need for a wide range of services is the general "charter school technical assistance organization" (TA). Every state with charter schools has at least one such entity, and many have more than one. Some TA organizations are nonprofit "resource centers" with business or community boards; others are membership associations, governed by charter schools themselves. These organizations tend to provide assistance to charter schools on the whole gamut of issues they may face. Charter schools call them with every question imaginable. Their annual conferences feature a smorgasbord of workshops on everything from facilities to curriculum design. They offer handbooks, newsletters, and Web sites that seek to address charter schools' concerns from soup to nuts. One, the California Charter School Development Center, offers "boot camps" for new charter school leaders, running them through a litany of topics.

As valuable as general TA organizations can be to schools, however, they often are not able to provide *intensive* services to very many schools. With their broad mandate to serve all schools and limited resources, it's not possible for most of them to roll up their sleeves day-in and day-out, or to provide them with full services, such as accounting or special education, the sort of intensity of service that is especially important in the start-up phase.

Several answers to the need for intense start-up help are emerging in the marketplace. One is the charter school "incubator," exemplified by the Education Resource Center in Dayton, Ohio. The ERC gets more involved in particular schools' start-up efforts than most TA providers, serving as temporary adjunct staff. It is also more selective. Like a venture capital firm, it carefully sizes up a client's prospects before providing help. In the small business world, incubators have succeeded but charter incubators are too new to show results. Another avenue is a growing number of fee-for-service start-up providers, such as the Minnesota-based nonprofit SchoolStart. Charter entrepreneurs contract with these organizations to provide all-purpose help in the start-up phase— help in preparing the charter application, writing the budget, finding a facility, selecting an appropriate learning program, and hiring teachers. The Education Performance Network (EPN), the professional-services affiliate of New American Schools, is taking a different tack by creating an "education management support organization." EPN offers clients a menu of services including data management, accountability and evaluation, education program design, and charter start-up and implementation. A key aim of EPN is to help build charter schools' capacity to manage themselves over time.

A third development is the emergence of leadership development programs for would-be charter entrepreneurs. Examples include the Fisher Fellowship program, allied with the growing network of KIPP schools based on the successful KIPP Academies in Texas and New York; New Leaders for New Schools; and the Massachusetts Charter School Resource Center's Leadership Institute. These organizations seek to provide in-depth training to potential school leaders, including both classroom and on-the-job components. Some follow up the learning with hands-on start-up assistance for graduates. KIPP, for example, deploys staff nationally to help Fisher Fellows get their schools off the ground.

Finally, several national organizations have begun to help their local affiliates start charter schools. YMCA of the USA is one. Another is the National Council of La Raza (NCLR), a leading Hispanic advocacy and development organization. NCLR has put together the most intensive package of services, including hands-on consulting for community-based groups starting charter schools, joint professional development opportunities, and the creation of national partnerships that can be useful to all the network's schools, which NCLR hopes will number fifty by 2005.

Diversity. Third, schools needs access to a variety of providers, so they can shop around for the best quality, fit, and prices. In contrast to district-based service systems, in which the central office or its chosen contractors provide all services to schools, the essence of the charter school service system must be diversity and choice. Schools must have enough options so they can voluntarily enter into service arrangements and hold providers accountable with the threat of exit. In addition to providing schools with choices, diversity would also help drive quality, as competitors vie to win business from choosy schools.

Types of Providers

Competition is growing and, across the different domains of service, many different types of providers are emerging.

For-profits. Although many of the pre-existing companies that have moved to serve the charter market are for-profit entities, numerous new companies have formed specifically to serve the charter market. One example is ABS School Services, an Arizona-based company that provides a comprehensive set of back-office services to schools, but there are many others focused on more specific areas or geographic markets.

Nonprofits. Many charter school technical assistance organizations are nonprofits, as are many other service-providers to charters. Even some organizations that charge fees for their services to charter schools, like SchoolStart and the Philadelphia area FOUNDATIONS, operate as nonprofits. Some of the most active lenders to charter schools have been nonprofit community development financial institutions, like North Carolina–based Self-Help and DC-based National Cooperative Bank Development Corporation.

Cooperatives and associations. Charter schools have also joined forces in some places to take advantage of the economies of scale attainable through joint action. Special education in particular has proved to be fertile ground for charter cooperatives, with models emerging in the District of Columbia, Texas, Minnesota, and Indianapolis. The D.C. Public Charter School Cooperative, for example, includes twenty-one member charter schools in the nation's capital. It aims to provide information to members about the complexities of special education, employ specialized staff that no one school would want to employ alone, and develop a Medicaid billing system to increase reimbursements gained by member schools. Charter school associations have also to a more limited extent played service-provision roles. The Colorado League of Charter Schools, for example, created a bond-financing program that allows schools with relatively small capital needs to access bond markets normally reserved for larger players.

School districts. Some entrepreneurial school districts have seen opportunities in providing services to charter schools. Numerous Colorado districts provide special education services to that state's charters. Other common district services include food service, transportation, payroll, and other administrative functions.

Nonetheless, for all the encouraging activity, the overall infrastructure is still not nearly as strong, nor as widespread, as it needs to be. It is spotty geographically: some areas are teeming with providers, others less so, and it is varied with regard to type of service: there appear to be plenty of textbook and software publishers, for example, but not close to enough providers of intensive start-up help. And there is a great range of quality.

There is also a cultural issue. Charter entrepreneurs are, by and large, an independent lot, skeptical of centrally provided anything. Many are fleeing from what they regard as overbearing bureaucracies, and they're not eager to re-enter a top-down system. They are inventive people, not inclined to buy something off the shelf. They shrink from talk of "systems" and "infrastructure." In short, the problem of charter school support services is not just a supply problem, it's a demand problem too.

Exploration of Scaling

Beyond building an infrastructure that makes it easier to start and operate a charter school, there is a second notion of scale— the idea that successful charter schools could spread their success beyond the walls of a single school. Education is notorious for single-school success stories that provide fodder for *60 Minutes* and feature films, but are never "replicated" elsewhere. Within traditional school systems, it's not hard to see why. Incentives to adopt good ideas from other schools have been weak, and constraints on change—from policy and culture— have been strong.

The charter school strategy has the potential to help overcome this conventional failure by providing a space within which it's easier to scale up what works via the creation of *new* schools. But to date, most effective charter schools remain single-site successes. Charter leaders have their hands full even several years into start-up. Their "model" may actually be heavily reliant on the personal leadership of one or more foun-

ders and/or local ties and circumstances. And charter entrepreneurs may see little incentive to branch out. Beyond the
intrinsic motivation to have a broader impact, there are few
inducements that would make replication worth the considerable effort involved.

Still, a small number of early successful charter schools are
beginning to explore scaling in one way or another.

KIPP. Based on the success of the two initial KIPP Academies
in Houston and the Bronx, KIPP founders Mike Feinberg and
David Levin decided to scale-up with support from the Pisces
Foundation and other philanthropists. KIPP's approach to scale
relies centrally on developing *leaders* to open and operate new
public schools, both charter and district-based. The highly selective Fisher Fellows program inducts twenty to twenty-five aspiring school founders per year and provides them with a summer
training program that includes classroom instruction at the University of California's Haas School of Business, half focused on
business matters, and half on academic and school issues. Fellows
then do a four-month residency in an existing KIPP Network
school. By spring, Fellows go to work founding their own new
school—with intensive assistance from KIPP national. Support
continues over three years, ending with an "inspection" to assess
how well the school lives up to KIPP's "five pillars," which are
the general principles that define a KIPP school.

By 2010, KIPP aims to have started a total of 200 schools
nationally. If successful, the resulting network will be an interesting model. It will not be an EMO—each school will be an independent entity, subscribing to the five pillars but individual—but
it will capture some of the advantages of scale, primarily in the
start-up phase. At this point, KIPP does not seem focused on reap-
ing other potential values of scale, such as the power of joint pur-
chasing or the centralization of certain routine functions.

Minnesota New Country School/EdVisions. Minnesota New ⌣

Country School in Henderson, Minnesota, is unique in two respects. First, its learning program is very unusual. Almost all its high school instruction takes place through personalized project-based inquiry, facilitated by teachers and relying heavily on the computers sitting on most every student's desk. More traditional forms of instruction come into play too, but only as needed to ensure mastery of basic skills. Second, the school is run by a cooperative of teachers, who make all the key decisions about the school—from the learning program to the budget to hiring and firing.

With funding from the Bill and Melinda Gates Foundation, the EdVisions cooperative is now seeking to spread its dual model to fifteen other new secondary schools over five years. Gates funding will go both to the new sites and to EdVisions central, which will provide intensive start-up assistance. Six sites are currently involved at different stages.

Expanding beyond a single campus or city, though, presents added challenges—challenges that so far have prevented most successful charter schools from seriously pursuing scaling. Again, what's needed is some new infrastructure that makes scale-up more feasible. Much of this infrastructure is the same kind of institutions discussed in the previous section—a diverse range of providers capable of helping schools with the whole array of service needs. If such a system existed, it would be easier for successful schools to scale up, just as it would be easier for brand-new standalone schools to start.

But there is more to the infrastructure for scaling up successful schools. First, successful schools need "diagnostic" help to know whether scaling up makes sense for them. Do we have something worth scaling? Is there a market for what we want to scale? Do we have the capacity to scale? Do we have the will to scale? How important are "we" to this? Can "we" be bottled? Schools need expert, distributed assistance to answer those questions.

In addition, schools that decide to expand need help in planning and implementation: What scaling model makes most sense, given the outcome of our diagnostic assessment? Should we actually try to own and operate additional schools that follow our model? Or create a looser network of schools, operated independently but following some core principles? Or should we scale up by offering training and consulting to other schools, or by licensing our approaches for use elsewhere?

What are the steps we should take to build the capacity needed to pursue that strategy? If we are "branching" in order to operate numerous sites, how will we provide all the services our network of schools will need? If we are forming a network, how will it operate? How loose or tight will it be? If we are using a training and consulting or licensing model, how do we turn our ideas into something that can be spread effectively through those means?

One possibility is the emergence of specialized "scale-up" organizations that provide these services to charter schools aspiring to have a broader impact. Such organizations could help schools determine whether scaling up makes sense, select a strategy, and develop an implementation plan. They could also offer specialized services like leadership recruitment, training, and marketing, that would be useful to many "brands." Right now, though, the catch-22 is that without the existence of such help, few successful charter schools appear willing or able to seriously consider scale. But without significant demand for help in scaling up, it is less likely that providers of such help will emerge on their own.

Implications for Voucher Programs

It seems inevitable that if the private school choice movement grows significantly, it will face many of the same supply issues that charter schools have faced. Existing private schools will be able to meet some demand within their current constraints of space and capacity, but a substantial portion of the new demand will need to be met by newly formed schools or by existing schools that are willing to expand or clone themselves.

Profit-seeking EMOs are an even less plausible solution for voucher programs. For one, voucher policies already attract more political fire than charter school policies in the states. A voucher movement in which many or most schools are operated by for-profit companies would be even more a political lightning rod and have even less chance of attracting bipartisan support. In addition, unless future voucher programs are substantially more generous financially than most current models, they are unlikely to attract EMOs to operate schools. Few EMOs are likely to be interested in serving a market where the voucher amount is, say, $2,500.

Much of the new supply, then, would likely have to come from the grassroots in one way or another. But as the foregoing discussion shows, this does not necessarily mean that each new voucher-accepting private school would have to go it alone. It is possible to imagine an alternative future, where the infrastructure exists to help make stand-alone schools viable and help successful ones scale up. The same kind of institutions that are essential for charter schools could serve private schools as well. In fact, one can envision an infrastructure that serves an array of school types—charter, private, and even district schools that have managed to secure some level of autonomy.

Factors That Will Help to Determine the Outcome

To be sure, the kind of future detailed above is currently only a possible one—not necessarily a probable one. A number of elements will help determine the outcome.

Investment. Some existing service-providers have moved

with their own capital to sell in the new-schools market. And even some new entities have been able to bootstrap themselves into existence out of the current revenues generated by their services. But many new service-providing enterprises will require substantial up-front investment in order to get off the ground. When the potential profits from a service are large and available relatively quickly, would-be providers may be able to find actual venture capital and other forms of private financing. Some other services, though, may require more time to show profits, or be only marginally sustainable even in the long run.

For these enterprises to obtain capital, more unusual forms of investment will be required. One potential source is private philanthropists who support choice. Though there are many ways such donors can back choice, investing in high-quality infrastructure would be a way to "leverage" funding significantly, by creating institutions that then go out and provide services to many schools. As Paul Hill writes, relatively small investments by private funders could create a workable infrastructure for new schools, paid for over time largely by fee-paying schools.[16]

Enterprise. Dollars alone will not build an effective support system for new schools. The key to an ever-improving array of options is enterprise on the part of would-be service providers. Creative thinking will be essential about questions like how to adapt existing services to new schools, how to use technology to deliver services across wide geographic areas, and how to keep costs down while still being responsive to schools' unique needs. Schools, too, must be enterprising—eager to experiment with new services, eager to let go of control of an activity in order to lower costs or obtain access to expertise.

Policy. State legislatures need to create policy environments

16. See Paul T. Hill, *Education Philanthropy for the 21st Century* (Washington, D.C.: Thomas B. Fordham Foundation, 2001).

in which new schools are viable. This means providing equitable funding, including facilities funding, so that schools can afford to purchase the services they need. It means maintaining schools' autonomy, so they can deploy resources as needed to get their jobs done.

If investment, enterprise, and policy can rise to the challenge, a very interesting future lies ahead for school choice—one in which the obvious demand for new options is met with a robust supply.

9

Implementing
No Child
Left Behind

RONALD BROWNSTEIN

The debate over school choice may be about to take a new turn. For years, reformers of left and right have dueled over whether the best way to shake up poorly performing public schools is to provide parents with the opportunity to switch to private schools (through vouchers) or to allow parents to move their children to better public schools (through public school choice). The federal No Child Left Behind Act, which President George W. Bush signed into law in June 2002, represented a victory for the advocates of public school choice: the law rejected funding for private school vouchers, but did mandate that districts allow children in persistently failing schools to transfer to public schools that perform better.

The law thus established a nationwide test of public school choice as a means of both providing better opportunities for individual kids and creating pressure on schools that are performing poorly. The results of that test are now coming in—and they don't look very encouraging. From coast to coast, school districts large and small report that hardly any students in failing schools are using the choice provisions of the federal law to move to other public schools. Even in some of the nation's largest cities, the number of kids traveling across town to attend better schools on any given morning might not fill a single school bus.

In part, the law's impact may be tempered by parents' inertia, lack of knowledge, or reluctance to upset routines and friendships by removing their children from neighborhood schools. Another problem is the sheer lack of high-quality public school alternatives within reasonable driving distance of a failing urban school; given the choice between the low-performing school in their own neighborhood and the mediocre school ten miles away, parents may stick to the path of least resistance.

So far there is little evidence that suburban schools are opening their doors to refugees from the urban systems. The federal law encourages such transfers, but does not require them, and most urban superintendents have found little enthusiasm for the idea among their suburban neighbors. In Dayton, Ohio, for instance, Superintendent Percy Mack says that he was turned down by half a dozen suburban districts when he asked them to accept children from the poorly performing city schools. "Basically what they said was they did not have space within those districts for any of our kids," he says. This is a problem familiar to education reformers: a voluntary twenty-five-year-old program that sends minority students from Boston to surrounding suburban districts has a waiting list that exceeds 12,000 kids because the receiving schools say they don't have enough space to accept more children.

Moreover, these obstacles are compounded by the fact that few districts are making it easy for parents to exercise their right to choose or to avail themselves of the related option that offers "supplemental services," such as after-school tutoring, to students who remain in schools that have failed to improve student performance.

Massive resistance might be too strong a term to describe the way in which local school officials are implementing these new options for parents. But not by much. Using both subtle and overt strategies, school districts of every size have made it difficult for parents of children in failing schools even to learn about the new choices, and they structured the programs in ways that make them less attractive to the parents who might be interested. "The only way you make something like this work is to fully inform parents what their options are and how to exercise their options, and school superintendents aren't doing that," says William L. Taylor, chairman of the Citizens Commission on Civil Rights, a liberal advocacy group.

The lack of enthusiasm, and in some cases overt hostility, toward the new requirements underscores the difficulty of implementing any reform that requires school districts to impose changes that challenge their bureaucratic self-interest. It also raises questions about whether public school choice, as presently constructed, can have anywhere near the impact its supporters have long hoped for. The coming debate will be over whether the solution is to create a more sweeping form of public school choice or to revive private school vouchers to create the alternative the public system has so far squelched.

Resistance Movements

The public school choice and supplemental services provisions of the No Child Left Behind Act were to be the most tangible lifelines for parents whose children attend low-performing schools. Schools that fail to make "adequate yearly progress" in improving student performance on standardized reading and math tests for two years in a row are subject to the

Act's sanctions. Their students must be allowed to transfer to a better school, with the school district paying the transportation costs. Alternatively, children who choose to remain in low-performing schools are eligible for after-school and weekend tutoring once their school fails to make adequate yearly progress for three years running.

This approach was meant both to widen opportunities for students and to place competitive pressures on the schools. Schools that didn't improve would risk losing students and the accompanying state financial aid. They would also be forced to divert some of their Title I money into providing transportation and after-school tutoring programs. This was supposed to give schools and districts powerful new incentives to improve.

Or to Resist the Law

In its first year, the transfer provisions of the new federal education law have had as much impact on the operations of the major school systems as a ping-pong ball fired at a battleship. In Chicago, of the 125,000 kids in 179 failing schools who were eligible to transfer to other public schools last September, less than 800 have switched. In Los Angeles, where about 200,000 students in 120 schools were eligible, less than 50 have changed schools. In New York, where 220,000 children in more than 300 schools were eligible, just 1,507 moved.

It's not only in the largest cities where the law has fizzled. In Cleveland, where 15,000 students in 21 schools were eligible, just 36 children requested transfers in the fall semester— and of those, nine eventually returned to their original schools. In Boston, where students in 65 schools were eligible, apparently no students have used the new law's provisions to change schools. Likewise, no students have moved in Dayton,

Ohio, though 10 of the district's 25 schools were on the state's list of failing schools. In Louisville, Kentucky, 2,900 kids in the Jefferson County Public Schools were eligible to transfer. Only 180 have moved.

What went wrong? The answer varies from city to city, though similar threads run through many of the tales.

In Chicago, local and state officials limited the program in ways that severely reduced its attractiveness to parents. Last summer, the state legislature passed a law saying that schools with selective enrollment, such as centers for gifted children, and those considered to be operating over capacity did not have to accept transfers from the poorly performing schools. (The federal law allows such exemptions so long as they were in place before July 1, 2002.)

Then the district offered transfers only to students in 48 of the 179 schools that had failed to make adequate yearly progress. All of the 48 schools were elementary schools. In the end, even with these limits, about 2,000 parents requested transfers, says Phil Hansen, the chief accountability officer at the Chicago Public Schools. But because of capacity constraints at the schools designated to receive the transfers, just 1,100 applications were granted. By the time school was under way, many parents had second thoughts, and fewer than 800 children had moved.

The Neighborhood School

For the city, Hansen says, the moral of the story was that most parents don't want to move their children from their neighborhood school, no matter how miserable its scores on standardized tests. "The lesson we learned, which we kind of knew already," he says, "is that Chicago is a city of neighborhoods. Parents take pride in their neighborhood school; even if it is a

low-performing school, parents feel closeness to that neighborhood school. What we heard from parents more often than
not is, I don't want my children to go to another school, but
what are you going to do to make my school better?"

Madeline Talbott, the lead organizer for Illinois ACORN, a
group that lobbies on behalf of low-income families, doesn't
entirely disagree. Parents, she says, are reluctant to send their
children to a different neighborhood, one that they might have
difficulty reaching in an emergency. But she says the way the
city limited the choices gave parents little incentive to accept
that risk.

"There were a lot of reasons we felt the way the thing was
set up was pretty useless," she says. "We felt the choice provision, at least here, was something of a sham. It was a very
expensive transfer of kids from one school to another that
wouldn't necessarily be an improvement and would not necessarily have the support of the parent."

The problem began, she noted, when the state exempted
many of the best schools in the city from accepting students
from the low-performing schools. The way the federal law
measures schools compounded the difficulty. Under the No
Child Left Behind Act, schools are ranked by the trend, not the
absolute level, of their students' performance on the standardized reading and math tests. That meant a school might be
designated "needing improvement" because it had failed to
raise scores over the past several years—but still could have a
higher absolute score than a school that had met the federal
standard because it had made steady gains from a lower base.
The result was that Chicago, in some instances, offered parents
a chance to transfer their children into schools whose overall
test scores were lower than those of the schools they were
already attending.

In the end, ACORN supported the city's proposal to limit

choice to just the 48 schools and to use most of the money that would have gone into busing to fund improvements in the failing schools. "If we could have constructed a plan that gave children in low-income, low-performing schools a real opportunity, we would have supported it," Talbott says. "But we looked and looked and could not figure one out."

The lack of better alternatives for parents in poorly performing schools may be an even greater problem in smaller cities. In Dayton, Ohio, the initial state review concluded that all 25 of the district's schools had failed to make adequate progress. After further analysis, the state concluded that test scores had improved enough at 10 of the city's schools to lift them out of that category. "However, those 10 schools resembled the 15 that did need improvement," says schools superintendent Percy Mack. "Some of them even had lower scores" than the 15 schools that remained on the state's list of failing schools.

In that circumstance, he says, the district decided that it made little sense to offer parents a chance to transfer their children to schools that were no better than the ones they were attending. It's a problem, he says, that is likely to be common in smaller and older cities. "In the major cities, where you are covering major areas of space, where some of the city schools extend out into the suburban areas, then you may find you have different looks and achievements in the schools," he says. "But in the smaller areas . . . you are going to see a lot of the schools look very similar."

Didn't You Get the Notice?

In New York City, the deficiency was less in capacity than in motivation. "There is a lot of blame to go around," says Eva Moskowitz, a centrist Democrat from the east side of Manhattan who chairs the City Council's education committee. "I think on the local level there really is resistance to embracing choice."

The breakdown began, she says, with the New York City Department of Education's decision to let each school district in the city decide how to contact parents about the option to transfer from poorly performing schools. Rather than writing directly to parents, she says, many districts apparently sent the notice home in children's backpacks—an excellent way to ensure that few parents ever see it. And for those who managed to fish out the notice from the swamp of old homework assignments, baseball cards, and snack wrappers in the backpack, the letters themselves weren't much more illuminating.

"The letter was not a particularly encouraging letter, and it was quite difficult to understand," says Moskowitz. "I have a Ph.D. in American history and I had to read it about three times to figure out exactly whether this choice was guaranteed, and who do I contact, and am I going to have to pay for the transportation? It also wasn't clear if I could pick a school out of my district."

As a result, few parents seem to have known about their options. A December 2003 poll by the Foundation for Educational Reform and Accountability found that 85 percent of New York City parents with children in failing schools were unaware that the schools were on the state's list of low-performing schools. The Albany-based foundation, which supports school choice, also found that 94 percent of the parents were "likely" to request a transfer if they were made aware of the option.

Even parents who understood their rights then found themselves confronting the labyrinth of the city's often impenetrable school bureaucracy. As in Chicago, "Parents who wanted a choice complained that the choice they were given had worse scores than the school their child was in," Moskowitz continues. "Others found that . . . if they had questions, and they wanted to see the school [available for transfer] they were told they weren't allowed to visit. The stories run the gamut, but it does seem there was either passive or active resistance to offering parents real choice."

Similar problems later resurfaced in the way the school districts notified parents of students who were eligible for the new after-school tutoring services established under the federal law. After the *New York Times* revealed in November 2002 that only 10,000 of the nearly quarter-million eligible students had signed up for the supplemental services, the city was forced to extend the deadline for applications. The problem, one city Education Department official acknowledged, is that districts did not want to lose the Title I money they would have to give to parents to obtain the after-school tutoring—and so did little to make parents aware of the opportunity. "Part of the problem is folks wanted to keep the money within the system," said the official. "Did the folks on the ground do an adequate job of saying to parents that the resources were available? The answer is no."

The breakdown in both the choice and the tutoring programs was so overwhelming that in December, New York City mayor Michael Bloomberg and Joel Klein, the new, Bloomberg-appointed schools chancellor, announced that they were taking over the process. Now, Bloomberg said, the central Department of Education would assume responsibility for notifying parents and establishing a process that would allow students in failing schools to transfer to better schools across the city, even outside their home districts. Watching the announcement, Moskowitz was encouraged but not entirely convinced. "I guess I am of two minds," she says. "It's hard to imagine it getting any worse. . . . Having said that, it's not as if the central [school administration] has any track record of doing this, or anything else, particularly well." New York City's intransigence even provoked a class-action lawsuit filed in January 2003 by parents claiming that the New York and Albany school districts had denied students their rights to transfers and to free tutoring.

New York was hardly alone in cloaking the new options. One potential reason that so few students transferred in Cleveland, for instance, is that the district didn't notify parents that the choice was available until four days before school began—at which point understandably few were enthusiastic about uprooting their children. In Los Angeles some parents were not notified until after the school year began. The breakdowns extended up the bureaucratic line; many states didn't notify cities which schools were failing until late in the summer, which gave them little time to contact parents. And many states were late in designating the firms that could provide after-school tutoring, with the result that districts, once again, had less time to notify parents. Illinois education officials initially told the Chicago schools they would not have to offer the tutoring services in failing schools until September 2003—which left district officials scrambling when the federal Department of Education decreed that they would have to begin offering the services early in 2003.

Not all school districts have been so resistant. Officials in Portland, Oregon, have gone out of their way to make parents aware of their opportunities. In October 2001, even before the federal bill had passed, the district sent letters to parents of students in three high schools it expected to land on the failing list, notifying them that the transfer option might be available for the next fall. During the summer of 2002, the district mailed a follow-up notice telling parents that the law provided transportation money for any students who wanted to leave those schools. Looking at test results in fall 2002, the district concluded that an additional middle school was likely to fall onto the failing list for the 2003–2004 school year. Once again, it notified eligible parents and urged them to attend an annual school fair where they could learn more about the schools available for transfer.

Yet even with this ambitious effort—which far exceeds the outreach in the vast majority of cities—only about 140 parents sought transfers, says Lew Frederick, director of information at the Portland Public Schools. The reasons that so many parents decided to stay put, Frederick says, include: loyalty to neighborhood schools; reluctance to travel long distances; concern about how their children might be received in a new school; the already available opportunities to transfer under magnet programs; and a desire to gain access to the after-school tutoring services that are promised to students who remain in failing schools.

The record is clear that most districts could make it much easier, and more attractive, for parents to move their children from failing schools. But the factors suppressing participation in Portland—which appears to have made a good-faith effort to implement the program—suggest that there may be a natural limit to how many parents will move their children from one conventional public school to another. The experience in Dayton, and to some extent in Chicago, defines another limit on the current programs: in many places, the schools that students can transfer into may not be enough of an improvement on the schools they are leaving to make it worth the trouble.

Turf Battles

In the months ahead, the limitations of the choice provisions established under the federal education law are likely to drive the debate in two different directions. From the left may come increasing demands that children in failing inner-city schools be guaranteed the right to transfer into neighboring suburban schools.

Faced with examples of suburban schools' refusing to take transfers, liberal education reformers are beginning to argue that suburban districts should be required to accept such children. In effect, they are using the logic of the education reform law to reopen one of the most divisive issues of the school desegregation era: whether largely white suburban districts should be required to accept black and Hispanic inner-city children. In the 1974 *Milliken v. Bradley* decision, the Supreme Court ruled that courts generally could not require busing across district lines to achieve racial balance; but the coming months may see more calls from liberals for moving kids across district lines to fulfill the promise of the federal law. "Choice within districts does not provide real opportunity to most of the students who need it," Goodwin Liu, a former education official in the Clinton administration, wrote recently, "The reality is that most high-performing public schools are located in the suburbs."

Conservatives take a different lesson from the disappointing results of the law's public school choice provisions. Many argue that the resistance from local public school bureaucracies shows that the only way to create genuine alternatives for children in weak schools is to provide them with private school vouchers. "There has never been more powerful evidence about the need for private school choice than the data that are coming out about public school choice," says Clint Bolick, vice president of the Institute for Justice, a conservative legal group. "In order to make the promise of No Child Left Behind meaningful, it's clear we have to look to every possible alternative, including private schools."

Some Bush administration officials are reaching the same

conclusion. Eventually, President Bush may use the bureaucratic resistance to public school choice to revive the proposal for private school vouchers that he dropped early in the negotiations over the education bill in 2001. "That's definitely something we have given a lot of thought to," said one senior official.

In the meantime, the administration is trying to nudge districts toward more enthusiastic implementation of the law. In October 2002, the federal Department of Education distributed nearly $24 million in grants to Arkansas, Florida, Minnesota, and districts in six other states to expand their public school choice programs. More important, last fall the department also issued regulations announcing that districts could no longer use a lack of capacity as an excuse to deny transfers to students in failing schools. That alone will require many cities to intensify their efforts. "We know we are going to have to be much more aggressive next year," says Chicago's Hansen.

Whether that will be enough, in Chicago and elsewhere, to provide real opportunity for children trapped in failing schools remains very much in question. Liberals and conservatives may not agree on the cure, but both increasingly believe that the federal law's current approach to school choice is fatally flawed. The cool response to the transfer option in cities as different as Chicago and Portland suggests that, whatever choices are offered, many parents would rather see money and effort directed toward improving their neighborhood school. However, parents who want to vote with their feet (as Ronald Reagan once said) may need more opportunities than the federal reform law has provided so far.

Freedom and Accountability

An International Overview

CHARLES L. GLENN

and JAN DE GROOF

The ongoing debate on "public" versus "private" schools is no longer centered on the right of nonstate schools to exist—a recent worldwide survey by the Organisation Internationale pour le Droit à l'Éducation et la Liberté de l'Enseignement found that only Cuba and Vietnam prohibit them—but on whether they should receive public subsidies to provide parents an effective choice of schools. A distinct issue, no less pressing, is the extent to which government may interfere with the mission and operation of nonstate schools, under a general theory of child protection or as a condition for financial support.

In recent years, there has been in most Western democracies a slow but very marked shift in the allocation of responsibility for the organization and control of education, in the public as well as the nonpublic education sector, through decentralization of various aspects of decisionmaking to the local school community. In some cases this shift has been motivated by concerns of managerial efficiency alone; in others, it reflects a deeper understanding of the appropriate role and, thus, the necessary *autonomy* of civil society institutions.[1] A distinction must be made, according to this view, between "vertical subsidiarity"—decentralization—and "horizontal subsidiarity" that recognizes distinctive spheres of responsibility.

While "autonomy" has become a fashionable watchword in education policymaking, there is also an increased stress upon accountability for meeting common standards. A new generation of education legislation in Europe, the United States, and elsewhere stresses core curriculum, common standards, and final attainment targets. This emphasis is combined with a growing flexibility in regulation of how schools achieve those results. As this policy shift has taken place, it has removed much of the reason for a distinction between "public" and "private" schools. If both are held to similar outcome standards, and both are allowed to organize instruction and (in some cases) appoint staff without external approval, the differences between the two sectors become less and less significant. This has been especially evident as new models of schools have emerged that are neither clearly public nor clearly private, such as "grant maintained" and then "foundation" schools in the United Kingdom, and "charter" schools in the United States. For such schools—and indeed any schools that are encouraged to develop a highly distinctive approach to education—parental choice is a necessity: children cannot simply be assigned to a school that has a distinctive character, nor can such a school flourish if parents do not fully support its mission.

This combination of school autonomy, external standards,

1. Gianfranco Garancini, "La dimensione giuridica dell'autonomia," in *Dalla legge 59/97 ai decreti-regolamenti: quale autonomia per la scuola e la formazione professionale?* edited by Gino Dalle Frate (Trento: Trento Unoedizioni, 1998), p. 18.

and parental choice has created a whole new set of policy questions. In a study of two dozen countries,[2] we have sought to understand the different answers that Western democracies have found to those questions.

Does the State Have an Obligation to Provide Funding to Approved Nonstate Schools?

The internationally recognized right of parents to choose nonstate schooling for their children has not, in most countries, carried with it an obligation on the part of government to fund that alternative schooling through providing subsidies to schools that it does not operate. Put another way, the allocation of financial resources to government-operated schools but not to alternative schools that meet the same conditions does not, under present international legal norms, constitute unlawful discrimination. While most wealthy democracies provide public funding for nonstate schools, they do so as a matter of a protected *right* in only a few.

The question of equitable financing of nonstate schools has arisen in many countries, once they are recognized by government as equivalent to its own schools and their diplomas are accorded official status in recognition that the education provided meets appropriate standards. After all, if a school is providing a public service for which funds are appropriated by the government, should it not receive a just share of those funds, based upon the number and type of pupils served?

While there is an issue of equitable treatment of *schools*, there is also an even more pressing issue of equitable treatment of *parents* who wish to exercise their right to make decisions about the schooling of their children. Obviously, exercising the

2. Charles L. Glenn and Jan De Groof, *Freedom, Autonomy, and Accountability in Education*, 2 vols. (Utrecht: Lemma, 2002).

right to education in other than government-operated schools will be financially impossible for many families if they must pay the full cost of that education. In addition to social injustice, the government fails in its obligation of neutrality toward religious and philosophical positions if it so organizes the educational system that there are strong incentives for parents to choose secular over religious education. The principle of strict neutrality insists that government should not seek to influence either positively or negatively the choices that people make "for or against any particular religious or secular system of belief. It should neither advantage nor burden religion."[3] A government committed to strict neutrality would fund equally qualified schools without regard to their religious character, and would demonstrate that it was strictly fair by favoring neither religion nor secular ideologies—nor the lack of all convictions.

The high-water mark, to date, in international recognition of an *effective* right to educational freedom, supported by an appropriate share of public resources, is expressed in the so-called "Lüster Resolution" of March 1984, in which the European Parliament stated that "In accordance with the right to freedom of education, Member States shall be required to provide the financial means whereby this right can be exercised in practice, and to make the necessary public grants to enable schools to carry out their tasks and fulfill their duties under the same conditions as in corresponding state establishments, without discrimination as regards administration, parents, pupils or staff." The inclusion of "educational services" in GATT negotiations could well lead to a generalization of this principle.

---

3. Stephen V. Monsma and J. Christopher Soper, *The Challenge of Pluralism: Church and State in Five Democracies* (Lanham, Md.: Rowan & Littlefield, 1997), p. 10.

Most Western democracies, in fact, have a tradition of educational freedom and maintain funding practices that encourage a great deal of diversity. There is a group of countries where the right to financing of nongovernmental educational institutions of compulsory education is stated in the constitution, explicitly or implicitly in the right to education and the right to freedom of education. The most notable examples are the Netherlands, where the constitution provides that nongovernmental schools be fully financed from public funds, and Ireland, whose constitution recognizes the right of parents to send their children to the schools of their choice and requires the state to "give reasonable aid" to private schools. The Spanish constitution opens the way to subsidy of nongovernmental schools by an "agreement" (*concierto*) between the authorities and the school. In other countries, public funding of nonstate schools has been established by law or by court decisions though not explicitly in the constitution. This is the case in France, where government enters into contracts with (mostly Catholic) schools to provide educational services. Public funding is also provided to approved schools in Austria, Belgium, Luxembourg, Denmark, Sweden, Finland, Norway, Iceland, Germany, Australia, New Zealand, Russia, most provinces of Canada, and South Africa.

There are also a few countries included in our survey that do not provide direct funding to nonstate schools, even while recognizing that they provide a service equivalent to that provided by public schools. These include Bulgaria, Greece, and (with certain exceptions) Switzerland, Italy, and the United States. The United Kingdom does not fit neatly into any of these categories. Protestant and Catholic schools have a strong presence within the public systems (an overwhelming one in Northern Ireland), but no public funding is provided to strictly private schools since the abolishment of the "assisted places scheme" under which scholarships were provided on a means-tested basis. The exception is the handful of "city technology colleges" that are legally nonstate though publicly funded. This brief description, however, does not do justice to the complexity of the arrangements, which include the charter-like foundation (formerly grant-maintained) schools. The question of government funding raises two subsidiary issues:

What Percentage of the Costs of Nonstate Schools Is Publicly Funded?

The amount of funds awarded to nonstate schools varies from no support at all to as much as 100 percent of the expenditure of public schools. In some countries there is a difference in funds awarded to schools that are religiously distinctive and those with a distinctive pedagogical approach. This unequal treatment has been appealed, unsuccessfully, to the European Commission on Human Rights. In a number of countries, the funding provided is in principle equivalent to the expenditure of public schools in the same circumstances. These include Belgium, the Netherlands, Finland, and several Canadian provinces (for Catholic school systems). In other countries, the public funding is set at some percentage of public school expenditure, with the difference sometimes explained by the greater obligation upon public schools to serve pupils with special needs. These include Austria, Germany, Sweden, Denmark, Ireland, France, Norway, Portugal, Spain, the United Kingdom, Russia, a number of Canadian provinces, two Swiss cantons, New Zealand, Australia, and (to a limited extent) Italy. Nonstate schools in the United States benefit from various subsidies for textbooks, meals, transportation, and teaching equipment, though not for operating costs or salaries.

Can Parents Choose Schools
Regardless of Family Income?

We were concerned to determine whether the various arrangements made it possible for parents of limited means to exercise the freedom to choose schools based upon their own convictions. Obviously, this does not necessarily follow from a formal right to establish nonstate schools or even from the provision of subsidies. Most Western democracies, as we have seen, provide public funding of nongovernmental denominational schools. The enrollment in these schools is either free, or—in case fees may be charged—the fee levels are limited or related to certain (usually marginal) services.

In a number of countries, tuition in approved nonstate schools is completely subsidized, but parents may contribute to the cost of education (typically, of supplementary services not provided automatically in all schools) on a voluntary basis. These include Belgium, the Netherlands, Ireland, Portugal, Spain, Sweden, the United Kingdom, Finland, and Iceland, and, in the United States, schools currently receiving "vouchers" in Milwaukee, Cleveland, and Florida. In Italy some nonstate primary schools receive a government grant that covers part of their costs and are forbidden to charge tuition, but they must make up the difference from "voluntary" contributions as well as inflated charges for services such as meals and transportation, which reduces their ability to serve families unable to pay a substantial tuition.

There are also several countries where nonstate schools may charge fees (even if they receive a grant from the state), but the fee levels are restricted or related to certain budget items. Because the German constitution does not permit any segregation of pupils based on parents' financial means, fees demanded by nonstate schools are moderate. Nonstate schools reduce charges to pupils of parents with limited financial means. In Luxembourg, the state takes responsibility for the range of operational costs not covered by fees. Fee levels are being kept quite low to prevent discrimination against children from disadvantaged backgrounds. In France, in the case of *contrat d'association* schools, families can be asked for contributions only for certain specified purposes: cost of religious instruction and ceremonies, sports or classroom equipment, or payments on the mortgage for the facilities. *Contrat simple* schools may charge fees for the costs not covered by government payment of teacher salaries. In either case, the school's contract must specify in detail and justify the costs that will be charged to parents, and this is subject to verification by government inspectors.

According to the Danish constitution, all children of school age are entitled to free instruction in primary schools, but at schools that offer alternatives to the public system there will often be a user-charge to supplement the state subsidies. In Norway, approved nonstate schools at the elementary and lower-secondary levels are funded 85 percent of the expenditure of public schools and those at the upper-secondary level at 75 percent. They are allowed to charge fees to make up the difference. In other countries, virtually all nonstate schools charge tuition and the amount of the fee is not restricted by government. These include the United States, Austria, Greece, Bulgaria, the United Kingdom, and Switzerland. Indeed, in all the countries that subsidize nonstate schools there are also tuition-charging schools that remain outside that system.

Is the Distinctiveness of Subsidized
Schools Protected by Law and Policy?

Public funding can become an "ambiguous embrace" that prevents schools from maintaining a distinctive pedagogy and thus also prevents parents from having actual choices, whatever the situation may be in theory. Although in most countries national education authorities still prescribe which subjects will be taught or attainment targets, there have been significant measures of decentralization in recent years, which has in turn provided more scope for pedagogical innovation. Policymakers are primarily concerned to balance the freedom of parents to choose a distinctive school with the right of each child to receive an adequate education, rather than to protect the distinctiveness itself, though obviously choice has little meaning if it is not among schools that differ in significant ways.

Nonstate schools—even if they receive little or no public subsidy—are typically forced to respect government regulations on curricula, attendance, admissions, quality assurance, inspection and control of accountability, the certification and employment of teachers and other categories of staff, and school buildings. This obligation is tied to the recognition of their diplomas and to compulsory school attendance requirements. Although in most countries national education authorities still prescribe which subjects will be taught or set attainment targets, there have been significant measures of decentralization in recent years, which have in turn provided more scope for pedagogical innovation. The primary concern seems to be to balance the freedom of the parents to choose a distinctive school with the right of each child to receive an adequate education, rather than to protect the freedom of the school to be distinctive.

Government fails in its obligation of neutrality when it imposes conditions upon religious schools that make it impossible for them to offer a distinctive alternative to a secular education. There are thus limits to the reach of government in seeking to promote, for example, its social agenda through regulating civil society institutions. "Courts essentially have said that states may not destroy the nonpublic educational sector by incremental regulation."[4] There is a growing recognition, indeed, that the school's own context, *its mission and culture*, the self-organizing and self-evaluating capacity of the school are all tremendously important elements in school quality.[5] Education authorities can be highly prescriptive. There is little scope to offer alternative pedagogies in Greek schools, for example; in Portugal, schools must implement national curricular plans (although government inspection of nonstate schools may not extend to the ideological, philosophical, or religious basis of the teaching); in Luxembourg, denominational schools (except the one Waldorf school) offer the same syllabus as the public system. The Swiss educational system, though under cantonal control, is generally one of the least flexible in Europe, with few opportunities to create distinctive schools and with a top-down approach even to pedagogical decisions.

Other systems allow subsidized nonstate schools to develop a distinct profile while implementing the compulsory national curriculum. This is true of the Netherlands, where nonstate schools have considerable autonomy to develop distinctive approaches to meeting the goals set by education authorities, and may define a distinctive character that government must respect. In Finland, nonstate schools can obtain approval to serve as alternatives for the years of compulsory schooling and the school may obtain public funding even though the curriculum may be significantly different from that prescribed nationally. In Sweden, nonstate schools can have a distinct profile and may comply with specific teaching prin-

4. Donal M. Sacken, "Regulating Nonpublic Education: A Search for Just Law and Policy," *American Journal of Education* (May 1988): 394–420, esp. p. 399.

5. R. Standaert, *Inspectorates of Education in Europe, A Critical Analysis* (Leuven: Acco, 2001), p. 115.

ciples or be denominational or specialized in particular subjects; subsidized schools must develop work-plans that illustrate how they will ensure that the national requirements are met. In Spain, schools are required to work out an educational project taking into account a required core curriculum; in some cases this direction-setting project is religious, in others pedagogical, and in many it is both. Nonstate schools in Australia have been required since 1999 to follow the curriculum framework established by the respective states, but a school may adapt or supplement the curriculum according to its specific religious affiliation or educational philosophy.

In Germany, nonstate schools must pursue the same objectives and provide a level of education similar to that of public sector schools, but are not restricted to the same curriculum. In France, the Constitutional Court ruled that safeguarding the distinctive character of a school under contract is required by educational freedom. Each intermediate and secondary school is required to develop and implement a *projet d'établissement*. Schools with a *contrat d'association* offer the same curriculum as the public sector. Those with a *contrat simple* must make reference to the curriculum of the public sector education. Unsubsidized schools must respect basic standards of required knowledge and skills. In Italy, the unitary character of the national educational system is protected through the national definition of curriculum goals, timetables, and specific learning objectives, but the curriculum laid down nationally may be supplemented with elective courses. Each school must develop an educational plan that serves as the "fundamental constitutive document" of the cultural and programmatic identity of the school and makes explicit its curricular, extracurricular, and organizational arrangements.

Yet other countries allow nonstate schools broad freedom to shape the education they provide. In Belgium, the government sets goals, but schools are free to determine the way in which they will reach them. In Ireland, the law gives explicit recognition to the need to protect the ethos of subsidized schools. Denmark has a long tradition of educational freedom; and its laws, policies, and practices encourage a great deal of diversity (based on denominational preferences, pedagogical theories, or political and social leanings), both outside the public sector and within it. In New Zealand, individual schools are allowed to develop a distinctive approach to education. In the United States, nonstate schools have broad—in some states, almost unlimited—discretion to shape their educational mission and choose their own standards.

There is, however, a further dimension to this issue of school autonomy, which requires attention and has become controversial in a number of countries. Most educational reform efforts in recent years have attempted to affirm the professional discretion of the individual teacher, so as to provide a significant measure of freedom to those in the best position to understand the needs of each child. This has been intended to raise the status and thus the attractiveness of teaching at a time when it seems more necessary than ever to attract highly competent individuals into the classroom. As the influential Carnegie report on the status of teachers put it, "within the context of a limited set of clear goals for students set by state and local policymakers, teachers, working together, must be free to exercise their professional judgment as to the best way to achieve these goals."[6]

However, pedagogical freedom is not limited to the individual teacher, but is also expressed at the school level, where the effort to provide a reliably and coherently distinctive

---

6. Carnegie Forum on Education and the Economy, *A Nation Prepared: Teachers for the 21st Century* (New York, May 1986), p. 57.

school may require some limitations upon the discretion of teachers. Parallel to the stress on teacher professionalism, there is a growing conviction that effective schools are characterized by a clear focus. The distinctiveness of schools may be described in terms of their internal organization or external context, but we are concerned here with something less tangible: the ways in which two schools that are formally similar both internally and externally may in fact function in very different ways and have very different results. Important as is the environmental framework within which a school functions, and the resources that it may devote to its mission, "a school's culture, or more specifically its climate, seems to be the determining factor in its success or failure as a place of learning."[7]

There is yet a third level of pedagogical freedom, that of the group of schools that seek to have an essentially common character in distinction from other schools. Montessori schools, Waldorf schools, Solomon Schechter schools, and—at least when a consistent effort has been made to realize a distinctive approach—Catholic and Protestant schools are not "on their own" but have a shared understanding of how their mission should be carried out. Formal or informal groupings of schools can be an important support for consistent educational pluralism, and governments in some countries—Australia and the Netherlands are good examples—acknowledge and negotiate with these intermediate structures. Although, under the international legal standard, everyone enjoys the freedom to organize education, the "organizing power" bears the legal responsibility for each school. In this sense, individual teachers have no "freedom of education," though of course (as occurred in Poland after the fall of the communist regime) two

---

7. S. C. Purkey and M. S. Smith, "Effective Schools: A Review," *Elementary School Journal* 83, no. 4 (March 1983): 427–52, esp. p. 444.

or three teachers may start a school and themselves become the "organizing power."[8] Many of the new charter schools in the United States have, similarly, been started by teachers, who thus possess the recognized legal status to control their schools under the terms of the charters issued by state and other authorities.[9]

Since every pedagogical situation is different, compulsory uniformity is most unsuited to good education. While central government is responsible for the provision of schooling, and thus for the resources required, for planning as needs and demands change, and for quality assurance, it is up to educators to take responsibility for the process of education. This requires that their responsibility be exercised within clearly demarcated boundaries, which nevertheless allow a school to manifest a distinctive character based upon its ethos. The ethos of a school, as we use the term, is that coherent set of beliefs about education, relationships, and the meaning of human life that underlies the character of some schools. In other—perhaps most—schools both ethos and distinctive character based upon it are simply missing, never having been thought through or considered necessary. The definition of their work is "based on decades of interest group negotiation and mandated responses to particular problems"; for teachers and administrators in such schools, "accountability means doing as well as possible on the statistics kept by the central office. It does not mean reaching and implementing a contract with individual students, teachers, or families,"[10] much less developing a

---

8. See the examples and discussion in Charles L. Glenn, *Educational Freedom in Eastern Europe* (Washington, D.C.: Cato Institute, 1995).

9. See Chester E. Finn, Jr., Bruno V. Manno, and Gregg Vanourek, *Charter Schools in Action: Renewing Public Education* (Princeton, N.J.: Princeton University Press, 2000).

10. Paul T. Hill, Gail E. Foster, and Tamar Gendler, *High Schools with Character* (Santa Monica, Calif.: RAND Corporation, 1990), pp. ix, 53.

coherent ethos to guide their practice. The character of a school that has a deliberately chosen ethos finds expression in the school's program of studies, rules for behavior, and expectations for staff and pupils. It is, to borrow a term from ethics, a settled disposition for the school to function in consistent ways.

In addition to its importance for school quality and for the satisfaction of the desire (and right) of parents for particular forms of schooling, the deliberate distinctiveness of some schools can have legal significance. The *caractère propre* or distinctive character of a French nonstate school under contract with the government has considerable significance as a result of the provision of law adopted in 1977 that teachers "are required to respect the distinctive character of the school" (*Loi Guermeur*, article 3). There is now an established body of law in Spain, Germany, Belgium, the United States, and the Netherlands, as well as in France, spelling out the implications of school distinctiveness, especially for personnel policy. A central consideration is always that it should be possible to substantiate in concrete terms whether or not the work of a teacher is consistent with the character of the school that employs her. This implies that character is expressed in clearly identifiable ways. A teacher could pay lip service to the ethos of a school, but there should in theory be no way to counterfeit compliance with its distinctive character—if that character has really been worked out in the details of educational practice.

It is coherency between the pedagogical project of an individual school and that of its "network," and, even more importantly, between the individual school's plan of action and the teaching style exhibited in classrooms, the messages communicated verbally and nonverbally to pupils, that makes pedagogical freedom a reality. In the practical organization of what occurs in a school, in the curriculum, timetables, teaching resources, objectives, evaluation techniques, and relationships among those involved, social and philosophical values and interests are expressed. Educational projects and educational objectives are not value-free, but are reflected in the organization and functioning of the school, all the more so since education is not purely an individual learning process but also a social phenomenon—part of the society that influences it and is influenced by it.

Belonging to a network of schools can be an important safeguard against subtly drifting away from an educational mission, as occurs with many schools, whether as a result of government requirements, of professional norms that influence teachers, or of the demands of parents who do not share the original vision of the school. Effective schools, while they are attentive to the concerns of the teachers and the parents at any given moment, are nevertheless also guided by a long-term sense of mission that cannot constantly be renegotiated and revised.

The freedom of a school to be distinctive, and of the sponsors or network of a school to be consistent about educational purposes, can be in tension with the freedom of teachers to educate according to their best professional judgments or personal convictions. A teacher participates in a school as an employee, with a set of duties spelled out (typically) in an employment contract, but also as a mediator—at least in theory—of the mission and identity of the school. The teacher-as-mediator is bound by a moral contract that cannot be specified in detail, but is of the utmost importance to her and also to the school and its sponsor. This situation to a large extent sets the tone for the relationship between the school management and the teacher. Importantly, it sets certain limits on the freedom to teach. One of these derives from the special nature of the profession, which involves working in the cause of the personal development of the young. Part of the teacher's role is to be an example of good character, of conviction, and of intellectual vigor, but in the exercise of that role he or she needs to exert the utmost care not to misuse the influence obtained on the minds of youth. Here we touch upon an issue about which it is difficult to be precise. After all, "the distinction between true education and indoctrination is one of the most important educational distinctions to make,"[11] and we cannot hope to add to a subject about which so much has been written by philosophers and psychologists. Nevertheless, the distinction is unavoidable, both for the school and for the teacher, though it has a somewhat different significance for each.

It is legitimate, both legally and morally, to organize a school around a particular educational mission; indeed, as we have seen, a school that does not have an explicit ethos and purpose that has been translated into supportive instructional activities is not likely to be educationally effective. For some schools (for most nonstate schools in most countries) an important part of that ethos and purpose is religious. Such schools seek to give children and youth a foundation in a particular faith-community through the content of the curriculum, the way in which it is taught, and the community life and ceremonies that form an important aspect of a good school.[12] Does that constitute "indoctrination," in the sense of an illegitimate manipulation of pupils with the goal of preventing them from thinking for themselves? Faith-based education may fall into indoctrination, of course, as may an explicitly "secular" edu-

11. Elmer John Thiessen, *Teaching for Commitment: Liberal Education, Indoctrination, and Christian Nurture* (Montreal: McGill-Queen's University Press, 1993), p. 18.

12. See Edward A. Wynne and Kevin Ryan, *Reclaiming Our Schools: A Handbook on Teaching Character, Academics, and Discipline*, 2d ed. (New York: Macmillan, 1996).

cation, but almost all religious educators would insist that it is their goal that their pupils think for themselves on the basis of a particular tradition, including questioning and criticizing that tradition.

Society is best served by a variety of communities, "little platoons" in Burke's phrase, within which loyalties and convictions can be shaped and moral norms internalized through example more than through precept. This is why "we need a plurality of schools, each beginning with its own conception of the present and the particular, but each also committed to fostering growth toward normal rationality and autonomy. . . . The best guarantee against institutional indoctrination is that there be a plurality of institutions."[13] International covenants and laws and the laws of Western democracies recognize the value of such schools, and most acknowledge that they serve a public purpose by providing public funding for them as well as recognizing their diplomas as equivalent to those delivered by public schools.

The teacher's freedom to express opinions, then, is limited by the pedagogical project that the school community has set as its goal. On the other hand, by becoming part of that community the teacher is more than a mere employee, and the school leadership has a duty to involve the teacher in specific aspects of working out how the school's freedom to educate is to be exercised in all aspects of school life. Freedom to exercise their profession supposes that teachers are partly involved in bearing responsibility for the school, a responsibility that they assume collectively.

13. Thiessen, *Teaching for Commitment*, p. 274.

Can Subsidized Schools Use
Religious Criteria in Selecting Staff?

Perhaps the most difficult issue in other countries, as in the United States, is how subsidized schools can retain their distinctive character while complying with laws against employment discrimination. Insisting that the rules and conditions of employment be the same for teachers in nonstate schools as for those in state schools could jeopardize the distinctive mission of the former. There must be room for additional rules for the nonstate school that complement the common statutory provisions that apply to all schools. Specific provisions must be in force between the organizing body of the school and members of its staff concerning specific incompatibilities and other issues in the light of the characteristics of the school's pedagogical project.

The borders between private and public law are becoming increasingly blurred. Authoritative voices in some countries argue in favor of abolishing national regulations for school staff, and the distinction between a statutory and a contractual legal position has become so small that the dismantling of the status of public civil servant as a possible strategy is being considered. The so-called "process of inclusion in public law" of nonstate educational establishments—stressing their contribution to the general interest (since they issue diplomas with effects in civil law, provide compulsory education, and substitute for the public system)—describes these schools as providing a *functional public service.* A period in which quite rigid regulations for state schools were applied with little variation to subsidized nonstate schools has been succeeded by a tendency on the part of legislators to leave ample room for customized staff policies, in both official and nonofficial establishments.

In many countries, the status of the staff of nonstate schools has become more "state-oriented," while that in public schools has become "freer." This shift in policies governing terms of employment has meant that the government stresses framework arrangements rather than detailed regulations. Such an "emancipation" of schools can lead to greater equality between public and private schools. There is, however, still a large variation among countries in the degree of centralization and government regulation of staff management. In most countries, although staff of nonstate schools must have the same formal qualifications as those in public schools, the nonstate schools have some freedom concerning recruitment of teachers and can require within certain limits that a teacher uphold the mission and the distinctive character of the school.

In some cases, private schools are not required to employ staff with the same qualifications—which, in practice, means the same formal training—as staff in public schools. The leadership of nonstate schools in Denmark is free to select qualified staff taking into account the schools' program and goals; nonstate schools may dismiss teachers if they do not support the mission of the school. In the United States, some states require private schools to employ state-certified teachers but most do not. Other countries require that nonstate schools employ staff with qualifications equivalent to those in state schools, but the schools may add other criteria related to the mission of the school. This is the case in Austria and Germany. In Belgium, subsidized schools have the right to freely recruit their personnel within provisions of the education legislation that provide general conditions for the recruitment of teachers with the necessary qualifications. Those requirements being met, boards do not have to explain why they have chosen an applicant and they may make decisions about employing and dismissing staff based upon the religious or pedagogical character of the school. In the Netherlands, nonstate schools must employ teachers who meet the standards for public schools, and they must provide instruction that is equivalent to, though not necessarily identical with, that provided in public schools. Teachers in a Catholic school, for example, must work loyally for the fulfillment of the goals of the school, including those reflecting a distinctive worldview. In Spain, nonstate schools have complete freedom concerning recruitment of teachers, limited only by the requirement that candidates hold the necessary qualifications for teaching a certain subject at the particular level for which they are appointed, as established for teachers in the public sector. In France, the director of a nongovernmental school may take religion into account in deciding whom to accept for a teaching position in the school, since she or he has responsibility for protecting the distinctive character of the school. The Canadian courts have upheld the right of religious or educational institutions to require conformity to beliefs and lifestyle standards on the part of staff. In New Zealand, boards of all schools have authority to hire teachers according to the particular needs of their school rather than having to accept whoever was sent by local government. Integrated schools (private schools that have joined the state system) are free to use religious criteria in appointing key staff. The issue has not yet been resolved in the United States.[14]

---

14. See Charles L. Glenn, *The Ambiguous Embrace: Government and Faith-based Schools and Social Agencies* (Princeton, N.J.: Princeton University Press, 2000), chap. 6, "Employment Decisions."

How Is Accountability
Provided for School Quality?

All countries in our study exercise some control over the quality of education provided by nonstate schools, whether or not these are publicly funded. Most provide for accountability through a combination of

- Prescribing the subjects that must be covered, and the hours for each, at each stage in the educational program, in publicly funded private schools as well as in public schools,

- Maintaining a system of school inspection, whether national or regional, and

- Administering, directly or indirectly, a system of examinations at the end of secondary education that have highly significant consequences for the future of students.

In general they do not attempt to provide for accountability through using standardized test scores to rank or rate individual schools (though England and many states in the United States do so), or prescribing books, materials, or pedagogical strategies to be used by schools. They vary in whether grade-to-grade promotion standards and graduation standards are set externally or by each school.

Most of these nations

- Pay for education nationally or regionally in a way that largely eliminates unequal spending on the basis of the relative prosperity of different communities but may also reduce local decisionmaking, and

- Provide additional funding to meet the needs of pupils who require more intensive educational services, often through the designation of certain schools or groups of schools as requiring a higher level of support.

School-level autonomy varies significantly among these nations. Most set standards for teacher qualifications, pay, and working conditions at the national or regional level, and these standards may apply to nonstate schools.

One of the most significant ways in which national policies differ is the extent to which hiring decisions are made at the school level. This can be a crucial issue for schools seeking to manifest and to maintain a distinctive character. Many require the sponsor, board, or staff of each school to develop explicit educational plans and assessment strategies, which serve as a vehicle for accountability in a context of autonomy. The provision, in most of these nations, of public funding for schools that differ from the state system in religion or pedagogy has the effect of encouraging philosophical diversity and school-level decisionmaking alongside a substantial degree of curriculum alignment. In some countries the overall responsibility for the supervision and inspection of nonstate schools lies with the central government. This is true of Greece, France, Ireland, Italy, Luxembourg, the Netherlands, Portugal, and New Zealand.

In other countries, the overall responsibility for supervision and inspection of schools is laid upon regional or local levels of government. The United Kingdom has three separate educational systems, covering England and Wales, Scotland, and Northern Ireland. In Belgium, responsibility for schools rests with the linguistically defined communities, in Germany with the *Länder*, in Spain with the Autonomous Communities, in Canada with the provinces, in Australia with the states, and in Switzerland with the cantons. In Austria, responsibility is shared among local, provincial, and national authorities. In most of the United States, the state government entrusts the supervision of private schools to local education officials.

There are also a few countries in which government exercises little or no direct supervision over schools that it does not directly own and manage. Denmark is the only country in our study that does not exercise control over the standards of teaching staff and teaching. Ensuring the quality of nongovernmental schools is left up to parents, who can select the person who will supervise their compliance with the quality requirements for public subsidy. Parents may also ask municipalities to perform monitoring functions on their behalf. Supervision of schools by the national government that funds them is concerned almost exclusively with the accuracy of their financial accounting, which is closely monitored. Legislation in 1999 established the Danish Evaluation Institute to provide systematic quality assurance and evaluation of all levels of education. In Sweden, there is no national school inspection system; subsidized nonstate schools are held accountable to the national curriculum frameworks by the fact that their pupils take national examinations at the end of elementary and lower-secondary school, and municipalities may inspect the activities of schools to which they award grants. There is also no national inspectorate in Iceland or in Norway, where school self-evaluation plays an important role in maintaining the quality of education. Australia has no formalized inspection system for nonstate schools, which may voluntarily participate in the Monitoring Standards in Education Programs.

Does Government Oversee the Teaching of Values in Nonstate Schools?

From an American perspective, the question of government involvement in nonstate schools may seem odd, though in fact much of the opposition to vouchers has warned that private schools might use them to teach racist or otherwise dangerous beliefs.[15] In most countries, in fact, it is generally accepted that subsidized nonstate schools have a right to uphold the religious traditions on the basis of which the school was established, but sometimes this is within limits. As we have seen, legislators and other policymakers have begun to think about education in a new way, less as a standardized product to be provided in a routinized way through bureaucratic procedures, and more as a diversified process responding to the infinite variety of interactions between pupils and those educating them. To put it another way, education is coming to be appreciated as a function of civil society (of the "third sector" or "mediating structures") in all its pluralism rather than of administrative rationality.[16] This new way of understanding education is accompanied by a recognition that it is inappropriate that "the state [has] an unchallenged monopoly on the generation and maintenance of values."[17] Government's task is not limited to the provision of financial resources to the organizers of education and to drawing up a regulatory framework for fiscal accountability. Government may seek to promote valid social goals through the educational system, though it should be noted that such efforts must be balanced carefully against the right of nonstate schools to represent to their pupils an alternative way of understanding the world.

For example, it seems well established that governments

15. See, e.g., James G. Dwyer, *Religious Schools v. Children's Rights* (Ithaca, N.Y.: Cornell University Press, 1998).

16. David Osborne and Ted Gaebler, *Reinventing Government* (Reading, Mass.: Addison-Wesley, 1992).

17. Peter L. Berger and Richard John Neuhaus, "To Empower People" (1977), republished in *To Empower People: From State to Civil Society*, edited by Michael Novak (Washington, D.C.: American Enterprise Institute, 1996), p. 190.

may insist that all schools teach in ways that promote respect for human rights, including the rights of women in employment and in citizenship, but it is not so clear that this implies that religiously conservative schools may not teach that women will achieve their greatest fulfillment as mothers. Here we have a distinction between a rule of economic and civic life, on the one hand, and a personal preference on the other; presumably it is not the business of government to insist that schools seek to shape preferences. Religious instruction as well as teaching from a religious perspective is accepted—often even required—in subsidized schools (as well as in public schools in most cases) in Austria, the United Kingdom, Germany, Finland, Sweden, Norway, Iceland, Greece, Ireland, Italy, the Netherlands, Portugal, Spain, Australia, Canada, and Russia. All these countries make provision for "excusal" or for alternative moral instruction on a nontheistic basis for pupils on parental request. In France, government funds the secular instruction in almost all Catholic schools, but the religious instruction is separately funded to preserve the official *laïcité* of the State.

A number of countries require that all schools promote certain values regarded as essential for a democratic society. In New Zealand, approval of a nonstate school requires that it "provides appropriately for the inculcation in the minds of students sentiments of patriotism and loyalty." In South Africa, schools have a major role in building societal consensus around a set of goals intended to promote civic peace and cooperation. The Spanish constitution requires that private schools provide instruction on the basis of respect for the principles of human and civil rights. In Sweden, private schools (whether subsidized or not) may receive approval only if the instruction they provide is based upon such democratic values as openness, tolerance, and objectivity. This does not preclude the school from having a confessional character.

May Subsidized Schools Discriminate on Religious Grounds in the Admission of Pupils?

Most Western democracies forbid discrimination on the basis of religion in the provision of public services, but the situation may be different when those services are educational and when some providers educate on the basis of a religious or philosophical viewpoint. In a number of countries, a subsidized school may use criteria for admission of pupils that are appropriately related to the educational mission of the school. In Austria, nonstate schools may select pupils based on the religion or the home language of the applicant. In Belgium, the school board can deny admission provided that the grounds are not based on improper criteria by which human dignity could be at stake, and nongovernmental schools can use religious criteria in admissions. In Canada, it is in principle accepted that Catholic schools give preference to Roman Catholics to give effect to their denominational rights, though many admit students regardless of their religious background. In Denmark, a nonstate school is free to determine what criteria to use in admitting and dismissing pupils. In Ireland, the Minister of Education is authorized to issue regulations governing the admission of pupils to subsidized schools. The Education (Welfare) Act states that the board of management of a recognized school "shall not refuse to admit a child as a student except where such refusal is in accordance with the policy of the recognized school concerned." For example, a Catholic school could decline to admit a non-Catholic child if a Catholic were seeking the same place, or if so many non-Catholic children had been admitted that the identity of the school were threatened. Similarly, in Australia enrollment preference may be given to a student whose family is a member of the relevant church or religious body. In the Netherlands, the board responsible for each nonstate school or group of schools has the authority to admit or deny admittance. In Germany, nonstate schools are in theory free to admit pupils who, in the school's judgment, are most likely to benefit from their program. However, it is forbidden to admit only children from wealthy families. In Portugal, nonstate schools have the right to decide whether to admit applicants, without any nondiscrimination requirement, and may adapt admission policies that give preference to children from specified religious denominations. In Russia, the admission criteria registration procedures are defined by the founder of an educational establishment in its charter.

Other countries do not allow such admissions criteria. Private schools receiving vouchers and public charter schools in the United States, if oversubscribed, must use random selection among applicants; other, unsubsidized, private schools may use any admission criteria except race. To be legally approved, a nonstate school in Sweden (whether subsidized or not) must admit all pupils who apply, within its limits of capacity, and they must be open to all and free of charge to receive public funding. In Norway, publicly funded nonstate schools must accept applicants without regard to where they live, and must accept any applicants who would meet the admissions requirements of equivalent public schools. *Centros concertados* in Spain must admit pupils on the same basis as public schools, without applying religious criteria, but in choosing a school with a religious *ideario*, parents are accepting the religious instruction and related practices on behalf of their children. In Italy, nonstate schools that seek recognition as equivalent to public schools must admit any applicants who are willing to accept the educational project of the school. In addition, extracurricular activities that presuppose or demand commitment to a particular ideology or religious confession may not be required. Finally, in France, the *loi Debré* explicitly forbids schools under contract from discrimination in admission. Although the school under contract may not seek to impose belief, parents who enroll their child in a nonstate school can be asked to sign a contract that requires them to respect the way the school operates.

May Parents Choose to Educate Their Children Exclusively at Home?

It is a common misconception that compulsory education also means compulsory schooling. In most countries, it is the provision of education that is compulsory—not schooling—and parents can provide proper education at home. However, in most countries (the United States is the great exception) only a small number of children are schooled at home for academic or social reasons. Home schooling is legally permitted and also monitored by education authorities in Austria, Belgium, Denmark, Italy, most of Switzerland, Iceland, Ireland, France, Norway, Portugal, the United Kingdom, Australia, New Zealand, Canada, the United States, and Russia. In Finland, the constitution provides that "Instruction given at home shall not be subject to supervision by the authorities."

Other countries in principle forbid home schooling but make exceptions in particular cases. In Spain, home education is allowed for children who would not normally be able to attend school, while in Greece, in the Swiss cantons Schaffhausen and Ticino, and in the Netherlands, home education is admissible for children with individual educational needs. Although the South African School Act provides for the reg-

istration of a learner for education at home, there does not
appear to be an express right in this regard. Finally, some countries—Germany, Sweden, Bulgaria—have compulsory school
attendance.

Conclusions

Educational freedom is one of the ways in which a society
provides itself with local institutions capable of engaging commitment on the part of ordinary citizens, especially parents,
creating the social space for institutions where children can be
nurtured on the basis of a coherent worldview of the sort that,
in a pluralistic society, no democratic government would be
able—should be able—to impose. If Montesquieu was correct
that "it is in republican government that the full power of education is needed," it is nonetheless essential that this power
be exercised in ways that are consistent with the requirements
of freedom and respect for the pluralistic nature of our societies. By making use of policies that permit and even encourage different means of reaching common educational
standards, educators working in nonstate schools (and in truly
autonomous state schools also) provide an opportunity for
themselves and for parents to exercise other essential rights as
well: freedom of conscience, free exercise of religion, freedom
of association, and freedom of speech. A diverse provision of
schools is thus a necessary response to the growing diversity
of cultural, worldview, and educational demands in a free society, and does justice to societal pluralism.

Educational freedom is not a matter simply of allowing for
or supporting alternatives to state schools; it also extends to
the functioning and influence of public schools. In a number
of countries it has begun to be apparent to legislators and other
policymakers that the inevitable communication of values by

state schools requires that the parents of the children who will be exposed to these values be involved with decisions about the curriculum and how it will be taught. The fact that parents have typically not chosen the public school that their children attend (in contrast to parents of children in nonstate schools) makes it all the more necessary that they have a voice in what and how the school teaches.

There are several current tendencies that appear in most of the countries covered by our survey. One is a greatly increased emphasis upon the autonomy of individual public schools, accompanied by an emphasis upon standards for educational outcomes. In effect, this is the "horse trade" proposed by Lamar Alexander on behalf of the National Governors Association in 1986: "We'll regulate less, if schools and school districts will produce better results. . . . [These] changes will require more rewards for success and consequences for failure for teachers, school leaders, schools, and school districts. It will mean giving parents more choice of the public schools their children attend as one way of assuring higher quality without heavy-handed state control."[18]

"Autonomy" is a constant theme in educational policy discussions, but it is usually closely associated with standards. As one might expect, the increased stress upon outcome standards has implications for publicly funded nonstate schools. As standards for public schools become more explicit and with heightened consequences, inevitably they are extended to their rivals—"free schools" as they are called in Belgium. This leads to the second tendency that we have noted: the distinction between public and nonpublic schools is becoming increasingly meaningless. As public schools enjoy more autonomy,

18. National Governors Association, *Time for Results* (Washington, D.C., August 1986).

and nonstate schools are subjected to more accountability for results, it becomes harder and harder to tell them apart. This is obvious when we consider charter schools in the United States. Although they are legally "public" schools, they operate very much like nonpublic schools, and are really indistinguishable from nonpublic schools in most other Western democracies: publicly funded, publicly accountable, nondiscriminatory, awarding publicly recognized diplomas, but owned and controlled by a nongovernmental board and free to express a highly distinctive educational character and to select teachers who support that character.

The time seems to be approaching when we will distinguish between schools that provide "public education," with public accountability, to any child whose parents accept the particular educational mission of the school that they select, and schools that do not do so. Schools in the first category, whether they are operated by local or state government or by nongovernmental sponsors, should receive public funding on the basis of the public service that they offer. This is already the case with privately operated hospitals, day-care centers, nursing homes, colleges and universities, and social agencies of all kinds. The religious character or the private legal status of these institutions have, rightly, not been a barrier to the recognition of their public contribution. The same should be true of nonstate schools, including those with a religious character, which provide public education that meets public standards. There will also continue to be schools that are truly "private" and that are unlikely to seek and should not receive government funding, such as elite independent schools.

Welcome as is the *Zelman* decision of the United States Supreme Court to those who care about educational freedom and social justice, it should not prevent us from continuing to urge that public policy be authentically neutral as between religious and nonreligious institutions, without requiring recourse to the excuse that the funds are passing through the hands of parents. Other Western democracies have not required that fig leaf, and it is high time for American public policy to grow up and fund public education in any school that provides it effectively and fairly.

Index